Infrastructures of Consumption

Environmental Innovation in the Utility Industries

Infrastructures of Consumption

Environmental Innovation in the Utility Industries

by Bas van Vliet, Heather Chappells
and Elizabeth Shove

earthscan
from Routledge

First published by Earthscan in the UK and USA in 2005

ISBN: 1-85383-996-5 paperback
1-85383-995-7 hardback

Typesetting by TW Typesetting, Plymouth, Devon

Cover design by Danny Gillespie

For a full list of publications please contact:

Earthscan
2 Park Square, Milton Park, Abingdon, Oxon OX14 4RN
711 Third Avenue, New York, NY 10017

Earthscan is an imprint of the Taylor & Francis Group, an informa business

A catalogue record for this book is available from the British Library

Library of Congress Cataloguing-in-Publication Data

Vliet, Bas van.
   Infrastructures of consumption: environmental innovation in the utility
   industries/Bas van Vliet, Heather Chappells and Elizabeth Shove
      p. cm.
   Includes bibliographical references and index
   ISBN 1-85383-996-5 – ISBN 1-85383-995-7
      1. Infrastructure (Economics)–Environmental aspects–Great Britain. 2.
   Infrastructure (Economics)–Environmental aspects–Netherlands. 3. Technological
   innovations–Environmental aspects–Great Britain. 4. Technological innovations–
   Environmental aspects–Netherlands. 5. Green technology–Great Britain. 6. Green
   technology–Netherlands. I. Chappells, Heather. II. Shove, Elizabeth, 1959. III. Title.

   HC260.C3V58 2005
   363.6'0941–dc22

                                                                    2005003301

Contents

List of Figures and Tables

FIGURES

TABLES

List of Acronyms and Abbreviations

CAT	Centre for Alternative Technology (Wales)
CFL	compact fluorescent lamp
CHP	combined heat and power
CO_2	carbon dioxide
DETR	UK Department of the Environment, Transport and the Regions
DOE	UK Department of the Environment
Domus	Domestic Consumption and Utility Services project
DSM	demand-side management
EESOP	Energy Efficient Standards of Performance programme
EST	Energy Saving Trust
EU	European Union
FSC	Forest Stewardship Council
GDP	gross domestic product
GWL	Gemeente Waterleiding (Water Company, Amsterdam)
Kg	kilogram
kWh	kilowatt hour
MAP	Milieu Actie Plan (Environmental Action Plan)
MRF	materials recovery facility
NGO	non-governmental organization
NRA	National Rivers Authority (UK)
OECD	Organisation for Economic Co-operation and Development
OFFER	Office of Electricity Regulation
OFWAT	Office of Water Regulation
PV	photovoltaic
PVC	polyvinyl chloride
TD	tariff differentiation
UK	United Kingdom
US	United States
WMO	Waterleiding Maatschappij Overijssel

Preface

In August 2003 an unexpected surge in electricity demand contributed to a catastrophic failure on the US national power grid. Such high-profile events serve as a reminder of interdependencies between households and the utility systems that serve them. Although we rarely think about it in these terms, each time we turn the tap and each time we switch on a light we are connected to an extensive system of provision, the tentacles of which reach far beyond the home. In this book we argue that supply and demand are intimately related. Utilities and users are bound by distinctive relations of co-dependency – relations that are, in turn, mediated by the technological systems and grids of which domestic infrastructures are composed. These interdependencies have important implications for environmental modernization and for the routes through which the provision and consumption of the key 'utilities' of daily life might be greened.

Our central contention is that the production of more sustainable systems of utility provision requires a transformation of collective social and material arrangements. In *Infrastructures of Consumption*, our aim is to show how infrastructural changes of this kind might be conceptualized and achieved. We use case studies of environmental innovation in The Netherlands and the UK as a means of exploring and illustrating the practical and theoretical challenges involved in renegotiating relations between utilities and consumers, and in redefining the part each plays in managing energy, water and waste. These cases allow us to identify new possibilities for the co-production of a more sustainable future.

Acknowledgements

This book draws on the ideas and results of a European Union (EU) research project entitled Domestic Consumption and Utility Services (Domus), which was funded under the Environment and Climate Research Programme (1994–1998): Human Dimension of Environmental Change (ENV4-CT97-0467). The authors would like to express their gratitude to the European Commission for this financial support. The authors would further like to acknowledge the major contribution Gert Spaargaren (Wageningen University) made in initiating and coordinating the Domus project.

All other contributors to the Domus project, including all our informants and interviewees in The Netherlands and the UK, are acknowledged for their support and views.

Thanks are also due to Fiona Summers for her work in editing the book.

1

Introduction

In a recent report, *Towards Sustainable Household Consumption*, the Organisation for Economic Co-operation and Development (OECD) showed how the environmental impact of household activities has increased over the last three decades and how it is set to intensify over the next 20 years. Some of the trends the OECD considers most worrying include the growth in household waste, increasing energy demand and regional imbalances in water supply (OECD, 2002). The OECD concludes that achieving environmental sustainability in households will require a 'shift [in] the structure of consumption' (OECD, 2002, p14).

In *Infrastructures of Consumption*, we show what might be involved in restructuring household resource consumption along more sustainable lines. The last two decades have seen a major realignment of relations between utilities and their users. Although numerous studies of social and environmental change in utility sectors exist, these have generally been one sided – focusing either on the macro-institutional transformation of networks, or on the micro-manipulation of household behaviour (Künneke, 1999; Ekins, 2003). Taking a distinctly different approach, we explore the idea that more sustainable systems of service provision suppose and require new contexts for the 'co-management' of demand *between* consumers and providers.

The concept of 'co-management' as it relates to the provision of energy, water and waste requires further explanation. Energy and water infrastructures actually enter and are part of the home. Although waste networks rarely involve quite so much physical interconnection, the activities of consumers and providers are interdependent, as when households separate waste to facilitate processes of collection and disposal. In these and other ways, utility consumers are literally plugged into the 'upstream' world of providers. These connections mean that action in any one part of the supply chain has implications for what happens elsewhere. This is demonstrated most dramatically in situations

1

of crisis or where resources are in short supply. In times of drought or fuel shortage, utilities often ask consumers to save water or energy, effectively engaging them as co-managers of the supply system.

Such arrangements illustrate the point that relations between the users and producers of energy, water and waste management have distinctive qualities and properties. Most obviously, they do not revolve around the 'one-off' purchase of discrete commodities. In the cases we consider, distinctions between supply and demand are often blurred: whether acknowledged or not, consumers and providers are both involved in managing flows of energy, water and waste. Just how this works out is of considerable significance for the reduction of consumption, for recycling and for the promotion of renewable resources. In what follows, we therefore address two central questions: first, how are social and material 'connections' or interdependencies between utilities and users changing; and, second, what do these developments mean for the construction of more sustainable systems of provision?

We start by taking stock of how commentators from the environmental and social sciences have conceptualized the consumption and provision of utility services. Taking further inspiration from social studies of technology, we explore the idea that relations between consumers and providers are constructed and mediated by suites of technology and that technical systems shape the dynamics of demand. We draw on case studies of environmental innovation with respect to the provision and management of household waste, energy and water systems in The Netherlands and the UK as a means of developing and elaborating upon different aspects of the consumer–provider relationship.

We focus, in particular, on:

- the differentiation of utility services (for example, the development of green electricity; grey water systems and multiple-waste streams);
- changing scales of provision (from pan-European networks to new forms of embedded generation);
- the experiences of individuals and organizations who have deliberately challenged 'mainstream' systems of provision; and
- the technological and institutional conditions and contexts of different forms of demand-side management.

In the process, we identify the potential for new types of 'green' connection.

UTILITIES AND USERS

Cohen (1998) concludes that the production-oriented ethos of environmental policy – one in which demand is explained in terms of population growth or macro-economic development – is giving way to a more consumer-oriented focus on issues of lifestyle, behaviour and individual choice. This shift is reflected in a number of contemporary policy documents. For example, a recent UK government consultation paper entitled 'Sustainable development: Opportunities for change' suggests that consumers have a huge impact on sustainable development through their influence as purchasers (DETR, 1998). Others point to the very wide range of activities through which consumers contribute to environmentally significant consumption. Illustrating this point, the OECD defines sustainable consumption as a set of choices relating to the 'selection, purchase, use, maintenance, repair and disposal of any product or service' (OECD, 2002, p16; after Campbell, 1998). By implication, the transition to a more sustainable society requires a sea change in the behaviour of individual consumers.

National and international policy-makers responsible for regulating the environmental performance of energy, water and waste utilities routinely suppose that the achievement of more sustainable patterns of consumption rests upon the decisions and actions of individual households. This kind of thinking has justified extensive programmes of social environmental enquiry bent on identifying the economic and psychological determinants of consumer behaviour (Ekins, 2003). Studies of this sort have, in turn, informed the design of policy 'instruments' intended to make consumers aware of the environmental costs and consequences of their purchasing decisions and lifestyle choices. Demand-side management programmes such as the UK Energy Efficiency Standards of Performance (EESOP) programme share this orientation.

Though dominant, this is not the only paradigm on offer. A number of social scientists have questioned the relevance of behavioural and individualistic theories of consumption and the policy approaches they support. Writers including Otnes (1988) and Spaargaren (1997) suggest that the environmental 'choices' of consumers are influenced by their attachment to shared social and collective networks. Taking a different tack, Shove and Warde (1998) conclude that it is difficult to make sense of the routinely inconspicuous forms of consumption involved in the reproduction of everyday life in terms of lifestyle choice or social differentiation. As these and other authors argue, people do not consume energy or water. In reality, such resources are used in the process of accomplishing normal social practices and achieving taken-for-granted standards – for example, of comfort or cleanliness. Demand consequently depends upon how these all-important services are defined and delivered and on patterns of resource consumption thereby entailed.

Different ways of conceptualizing consumption have practical consequences for the design and development of environmental policy. As we have already seen, many commentators equate sustainable consumption with the production and promotion of ecological products and services (Ekins, 2003). For Mol and Spaargaren (1992), the sustainable transformation of domestic practices requires 'bottom-up' consumer activism in combination with a 'top-down' greening of supply chains. Instead of taking present levels of demand for granted, other commentators argue that environmental policy should seek to challenge assumptions, commitments and conventions around which ordinary consumption is organized (Redclift, 1996; Shove, 2003).

This book explores the relevance of debates such as these for the analysis and interpretation of the changing relationship between utilities and their users.

INFRASTRUCTURES AND ENVIRONMENTAL INNOVATION

As we have already noticed, the provision and consumption of energy and water and the management of waste is mediated and structured by all manner of technological systems. In practice, the actions and inactions of individual households are rather directly dependent upon a variety of mediating devices and upon the infrastructures to which they are attached (Otnes, 1988). Contemporary routines of washing and bathing suppose the existence of taps, showers and sinks. Likewise, using electricity is impossible in the absence of things such as light bulbs, vacuum cleaners, washing machines, heaters and computers. At the same time, none of the activities mentioned above would be possible without a wider infrastructure of supply comprising transmission lines, sub-stations, reservoirs and disposal sites.

Environmental policy-makers who view sustainable consumption as an expression of individual choice generally focus on isolated technical fixes – for example, on the acquisition of more efficient freezers, light bulbs or heating systems. These 'solutions' allow people to maintain current lifestyles and social practices but with fewer resources. What is missing here is an analysis of the co-evolution of technology and practice – for instance, of how freezers structure and are structured by systems of food provisioning. Throughout this book we illustrate the extent to which consumption practices are shaped by the distinctive socio-technical systems upon which they depend.

Increasing the efficiency of domestic technology makes it possible to get more from a given amount of water or electricity (von Weizsäker et al, 1998). But however efficient, such technologies may also increase demand for services and/or promote ultimately unsustainable patterns of waste production. In other words, there are different ways in which technical infrastructures structure the resource intensity of everyday life. The household dustbin is, for instance, more than just a receptacle for waste. Its size and design permit certain practices and prevent others. These characteristics do not arise by accident. As Chappells and Shove (1999) argue, they are the physical embodiment of an institutional relationship between the household and those who collect the rubbish. To borrow terms developed by Akrich (1992) and Latour (1992), energy- and water-consuming appliances, such as the dustbins referred to above, are 'inscribed' with meanings, assumptions and rule sets. Scripts do not determine the processes and practicalities of use; but household technologies are, nonetheless, implicated in mediating relations between utility consumers and providers and in creating particular contexts for environmental action.

It is important to think about how mediating technologies structure the ways in which consumers use, store and dispose of resources. But as Otnes (1988) observes, households are part of a more extensive socio-material system in which yet other technologies are involved in processes of generation, distribution, storage and treatment. The design and management of these socio-technical complexes is itself of consequence for the timing and intensity of resource flows and, hence, for the dynamics of household demand. Various authors have written about how large technical systems come to be as they are and about the political, organizational and operational norms they embody (Hughes, 1983; Coutard, 1999; Moss, 2004). For example, Hughes explains that power networks built to meet universal needs perpetuate a 'predict-and-provide' culture that is at odds with the systematic and careful management of demand (Hughes, 1983). Although infrastructural hardware is relatively durable (in the form of pumping stations, sewerage systems, power plant, etc.), the institutional environment is more fluid. Writers such as Coutard (1999), Guy and Osborn (1997) and Summerton (1994) claim that new regimes of ownership and management generate new priorities and objectives, the realization of which has practical consequences for the ways in which networks are managed and developed.

Together, these observations suggest that institutions and infrastructures actively create and structure contemporary patterns of demand. Taking these points on board, the challenge of engendering more sustainable forms of energy, water and waste management is one of reconfiguring these arrangements as well as (and as part of) shifting consumers' habits and practices. Drawing on these ideas, this book recognizes the many scales and levels at which past and present systems of energy, water and waste management influence the actions of today's consumers and providers and, hence, the potential for 'greening' connections between utilities and their users.

ENERGY, WATER AND WASTE: CHARACTERISTICS AND DYNAMICS

Fine and Leopold (1993) argue that attempts to analyse and explain patterns of consumption should take account of the unique characteristics and dynamics of commodity-specific 'systems of provision'. Energy (by which we mostly mean electricity), water and waste have distinctive material properties. Most obviously, electricity is invisible and cannot be stored as easily as water or waste. Meanwhile, there are different qualities and grades of water and waste, and different ways of managing their separation, storage and treatment. In what follows we take note of these material features and what they mean for the dynamics of consumption and provision.

These differences aside, the continuous provision of energy, water and waste management is now regarded as essential for modern life. Partly because systems of public provision are already well established (many date from the 19th century), the ways in which infrastructures shape demand and consumer practice have faded from view. Consumers are only dimly aware of the social and technical systems and of the miles of wires and pipes upon which their routines depend. Having said that, in the UK and The Netherlands, as elsewhere, the utilities remain politically important for the social and economic development of the nation as a whole. Because of this, their organization and operation is not left to commercial interests alone. Even though the provision of these once public goods is now framed by a political economy of privatization and liberalized market arrangements, the utilities are closely regulated. Relations between utilities and their users, and between utilities and the technological systems for which they are responsible are, in turn, structured by an array of national and increasingly transnational regulatory regimes. These are of some consequence for the possibilities and practicalities of environmental reform.

To summarize, energy, water and waste networks share a number of distinctive characteristics. Consumers and providers are interdependent in rather special ways. As owners of the sensitive fingertips of the infrastructure itself (i.e. the home), consumers are directly implicated in the functioning of the system as a whole. Second, consumption is mediated by a set of intervening devices (showers, toasters, freezers etc.), the design, ownership and use of which determines changing patterns of demand. Third, the wider infrastructure, in the form of reservoirs, power plant, distribution systems etc., has qualities and properties that make a real difference to the management and flow of resources behind the scenes. Fourth, methods of management and patterns of future investment reflect institutional and regulatory regimes, many of which have changed dramatically during recent years. Finally, the resources we consider have specific material properties. These make a difference to the manner in which they are generated, delivered and used.

THEMES, QUESTIONS AND METHODS

Having set out some of the main features of our approach, we now elaborate on the central themes around which this book is organized. In one way or another, the four themes outlined below deal with the basic question of what changing systems of utility provision mean for the possibilities and prospects of sustainability.

Differentiation and choice

Utilities – as state monopolies – have traditionally provided an undifferentiated service, delivering 'standard' energy, supplying drinking-quality water and removing all waste. Consumers were 'captive' in the sense that they had no option but to connect to the network of the provider operating in their area. In many European countries, publicly owned monopolies have been privatized and markets opened up to competition. Partly, but not only, as a result of these developments, services and resources are not as uniform as they once were. In looking for ways to compete and segment markets, certain utility providers are exploring ways of developing and promoting specifically 'green' products and services. Does this mean that consumers can, at last, give expression to their green commitments and opt for 'the environment' as their brand of choice? More generally, what do new processes of differentiation – for instance, between 'green' and brown electricity, between different waste streams and different qualities of water – mean for the infrastructure as a whole?

Proponents of privatization generally argue that market liberalization 'empowers' consumers and offers them greater choice of service providers, products and tariffs (Awerbuch, 2003). Others are more sceptical. Summerton, for one, draws attention to the socially divisive character of service restructuring in the electricity sector and to the new 'haves and have-nots' of utility provision (Summerton, 2004). In what follows, we conclude that the representation of utility consumers as either 'autonomous' or 'captive' overlooks subtle but important distinctions in the (indirect) part that *different* consumers play in the management and operation of utility systems. The cases we consider illustrate the multiple ways in which consumer–provider relations are being reconfigured. Rather than observing a swing from captive to authoritative consumer, we detect a proliferation of new arrangements, each affording different degrees of 'autonomy' from mainstream provision and each generating specific opportunities for demand management and environmental innovation.

Scales and sites of change

From the early 1970s on, questions of scale have played an important part in debates about the qualities and characteristics of sustainable energy, water or waste infrastructures. What are the relative economic and environmental costs and benefits of 'small-scale' versus 'large-scale' systems and of 'top-down' or 'bottom-up' modes of organization (Schumacher, 1973)? In other words, is small really beautiful? Again, contemporary theories of infrastructural change suggest that it is not a matter of choosing between large or small: instead, the challenge is to understand how multiple modes of organization interact (von Meier, 1994; Graham and Marvin, 2001). Guy and Marvin (1995) describe the development of coexisting modes of utility organization, each taking place on a different social, technical or spatial scale. These authors conclude that each such arrangement generates its own logic of service provision and demand management. Similar patterns are evident in the cases we examine.

New modes of 'sustainable' provision

We have argued above that there is a close relation between ordinary domestic technology, the infrastructures upon which these devices depend and the routines and practices of those who use them. By implication, new modes of sustainable provision suppose somewhat different routines and practices, and somewhat different relations between utilities and users. We studied nine 'sustainable' housing projects deliberately designed and managed with environmental innovation in mind. In analysing these cases, some from The Netherlands, some from the UK, we describe their social, technical and institutional organization in some detail. We conclude that novel, non-mainstream arrangements generate different opportunities for demand management. However, we also notice a persistent dependence upon certain forms of centralized provision. Again, it is not so much a matter of being 'on' or 'off' grid, but of negotiating different combinations and configurations of supply and demand.

Restructuring demand and efficiency

Given the economic, not to mention environmental, problems of continuing to expand supply – to build new reservoirs, power stations and waste management facilities – strategies of 'demand-side management' make increasing sense. If they can reduce or change the timing of demand, utilities can continue to provide services, but without having to invest in new capacity. There are many different reasons why utilities might want to manage demand; but some have to do with the scale and interconnectedness of the grids involved. Where networks (e.g. power grids or watercourses) are small, the challenges of balancing supply and demand are often more pronounced. Bounded infrastructures have limited capacity (there is a ceiling of supply) and limits as to how much demand can be met. In discussing the practicalities of demand-side management with respect to waste, energy and water, we take further issues already touched upon in our discussions of scale and of new modes of provision. We analyse demand management in such a way as to highlight connections between the micro-level restructuring of household systems of energy, water or waste management and the macro-level restructuring of institutions and infrastructures.

Methods

This book is unusual in that it deals with energy, waste and water. It does so partly because all are important for environmental sustainability, because all constitute 'networked' forms of infrastructural provision, and because all have been subject to similar forms of institutional change during recent years. As well as acknowledging the very important material differences between these resources (for instance, in terms of visibility, storage, hazard, etc.), we take the chance to compare and draw parallels between systems that are more commonly analysed in isolation.

Our second axis of comparison is between the UK and The Netherlands. These two countries now have much in common – for instance, in terms of gross domestic product (GDP), standards of housing and certain relevant features of culture. Yet, they have somewhat different histories of infrastructural provision – especially with respect to the role of the state. In what follows, we play down occasionally important features of national difference in order to highlight common trends and tendencies. This is more a study of the qualities and characteristics of infrastructural provision than of UK utilities compared to those of The Netherlands. However, experiences from the two countries provide useful and often relevant reminders of the historical and cultural specificity of much of what we describe.

In detail, the research upon which we draw involved a number of steps. The first was to identify, catalogue and analyse examples of 'environmental innovation'. By this we mean innovation whether of technology, process or institutional arrangement, explicitly undertaken in the name of sustainability. The 150 cases represented in the resulting inventory include instances of waste separation, of photovoltaic technologies, wind power, local hydro systems, composting toilets, reed-bed sewerage systems, and more.[1] Furthermore, interview-based research was undertaken to better understand the issues involved in developing and managing a sample of these cases. Examples were selected for further investigation on the grounds that they required some renegotiation of relationships between utilities and consumers. This strategy means that the empirical material we discuss in the following chapters is drawn from what we might think of as 'extreme' cases involving purposeful environmental innovation and some more or less deliberate challenge to mainstream provision. The patterns we describe are not necessarily universal; but by looking at instances that fit these criteria, we are able to see what is involved in making new, deliberately green, connections.

ORGANIZATION OF THE BOOK

Chapter 2, 'Linking Utilities and Users', reviews different ways of conceptualizing relations between the consumers and providers of electricity, water and waste services. Distinctions are drawn between approaches that focus on individual consumers as the agents of environmental change and those that consider sustainability to be a matter for collective or social transformation.

Chapter 3, 'Infrastructural Change and Sustainable Consumption', takes stock of the technical and institutional histories of energy, waste and water infrastructures in the UK and The Netherlands. In this chapter we describe how different priorities and logics of provision have gained favour at different moments in the history of these two countries, how these have influenced the social and technical structures of today, and what this means for demand in each sector.

The remainder of the book makes use of specific cases of innovation in energy, water and waste management as a means of elaborating on the four themes outlined above.

Chapter 4, 'Differentiation and Choice in Water, Electricity and Waste Services', examines some of the more 'conspicuous' aspects of network change for household consumers. The liberalization and deregulation of markets has facilitated the entry of many new provider organizations and service options. Has this enhanced opportunities for consumers to act as environmentally conscious demand managers? The profusion of recycling bins, green electricity schemes and (in some situations) possibilities for using different grades of water to drink, bathe or flush toilets suggests that this may be the case. But to what extent are these merely 'cosmetic' changes? What do they mean for the more or less sustainable character of the entire system of provision? Decisions about whether to buy green electricity or take cans to the recycling bin require one type of socio-technical response; but other forms of environmental innovation demand a more extensive reconfiguration of utility–user relations and household infrastructures.

In examining 'scales of provision', Chapter 5, 'Shifting Scales and the Co-production of Green Grids', revisits arguments about whether 'bottom-up' or 'top-down' models of network organization are environmentally optimal. We show that a variety of socio-technical constellations, featuring both centralized and decentralized components, can engender more sustainable patterns of consumption.

Chapter 6, 'New Modes of "Sustainable" Provision', reviews the experiences of households that have sought to disconnect from mainstream grids and establish their own electricity, water and waste systems. How, and how far, have those involved managed to reconfigure 'normal' social and technical dependencies? The autonomous 'off-grid' and semi-autonomous arrangements we describe, again, suggest that there are multiple opportunities for configuring more sustainable household infrastructures.

Efforts to reconnect demand to supply management have been a key component of utility reforms since the early 1990s. Chapter 7, 'Restructuring Demand and Efficiency', takes stock of what has been achieved so far and suggests that contemporary models of demand management fail to engage consumers as partners in sustainable provision.

Finally, Chapter 8, 'Systems of Provision and Innovation', draws these themes and dimensions together. Reflecting upon the new network arrangements we have found, we identify different forms of socio-technical connectivity and show what these mean for the greening of relations between utilities and users. In conclusion, we explain why the concept of 'co-provision' is so important in understanding the challenges involved in establishing green connections.

NOTE

1 The full catalogue of 150 cases includes instances from The Netherlands, the UK and Sweden. The inventory was compiled for the Domus project (see Raman et al, 1998).

2

Linking Utilities and Users

The title of this chapter serves multiple purposes. It is partly an injunction: a reminder that providers and consumers are jointly implicated in the management of waste, energy and water. It is also an intellectual ambition. As we explain in this chapter, new tools and resources are required to conceptualize and analyse changing relations between utilities and users.

Energy and water consumption and waste management have significantly different qualities as 'environmental' issues. Given current forms of generation, escalating demand for energy – and, in particular, for electricity – has rather direct consequences for carbon dioxide (CO_2) emissions and hence for global warming. The environmental impacts of water consumption are often more obviously local since they are to do with the relation between abstraction and changing ecosystems. As with electricity, much depends upon the nature of the infrastructure and associated possibilities for managing distribution and flow. Meanwhile, waste can constitute all manner of environmental 'problems', depending upon the properties and the volume of the stuff itself. More abstractly, waste counts as an environmental issue not simply because of toxicity or degradation, but because it signifies profligacy and the unsustainable consumption of non-renewable resources.

By bundling these diverse concerns together, conventional definitions of sustainable development as that which 'meets the needs of the present without compromising the ability of future generations to meet their own needs' (WCED, 1987, p43) treat 'the environment' as one. Consistent with this approach, policies to promote sustainable consumption are generally designed to reduce the size of the ecological footprints associated with contemporary forms of consumer behaviour (Wackernagel and Rees, 1995). Strategies of this kind almost always focus on the actions and decisions of individual consumers. Having defined the problem – and the solution – in terms of consumer choice, the central policy challenge is that of persuading people to make 'the environment' their preferred brand and to opt for goods and services that are less resource intensive to provide.

As these paragraphs imply, 'the consumer' and 'the environment' are constructed in ways that have far-reaching but often unintended consequences for the conceptualization of sustainability and for the sorts of initiatives developed in its name. One purpose of this chapter is to revisit dominant theories of 'green' consumption in order to show how well, and how badly, they apply to the use of energy and water and the management of waste. This is an important task. If energy, water and waste really are vital environmental issues, failure to adequately conceptualize their consumption represents a serious problem for those seeking to reduce demand.

It is immediately apparent that 'the utilities' have certain distinctive qualities. One is the extent to which we have become dependent upon their consistent and reliable supply. As Hutton explains, major power failure 'rams home to ordinary people what otherwise exists only as a theory. Electricity is not a commodity like a designer dress where an interruption of supply poses no wider consequences; it is a precondition for successful modern life' (Hutton, 1998, p24). More ordinarily, but just as important, forms of energy and water consumption are routinely invisible. There are two aspects to this. One is that utility bills come but once a quarter and it is by then impossible to relate the levels of consumption shown to the past practices that occasioned them. The other is that resources are consumed not for their own sake, but in the course of achieving services such as those of heating, bathing, lighting, cooling etc. The use of energy and water is consequently mediated by a battery of intervening technologies (baths, light bulbs, boilers), and by an array of social and cultural norms and conventions, including those of comfort, cleanliness and convenience. In addition, and as we explain below, relationships between supply and demand are complicated and co-constitutive. As a result, the manner in which resources are provided is itself important for ensuing patterns of consumption.

In this chapter, and in the book as a whole, we investigate the relationship between consumption and provision, focusing on the consequences that changing systems of provision (notably from monopoly providers to competition in liberalized markets) might have for energy and water demand and for the management of waste. In principle, organizational transformations generate new and different possibilities for environmental reform. For example, it is now possible to imagine the development of highly localized systems of embedded generation and of massive pan-European networks, neither of which were easy to picture under conditions of national monopoly. Rather than focusing on the technological efficiencies of one scenario or another, we argue that the environmental implications of institutional change depend upon the relation between provision (supply) and consumption (demand), and upon the links that are forged and broken between utilities and their users.

The rest of this chapter makes the case for re-conceptualizing the relation between provision and consumption – and, in particular, the consumption of domestic utilities. Critically, we argue that patterns of consumption follow from and reflect the effective accomplishment of what people take to be normal routines and practices. We make the further claim that understandings of normal and ordinary routines change in ways that are at least partly related to the systems and technologies through which they are defined, delivered and provided. Equally, models of need and assumptions about demand are quite literally built into networks and infrastructures of provision. Though invisible to any one end user, such assumptions are, nonetheless, important in establishing, challenging and stabilizing demand.

The idea that systems of provision and patterns of consumption constitute each other has important implications when thinking about the practical, cultural and political implications of institutional change. We discuss the differentiation of energy, water and waste and the production of multiple varieties of each in terms of newly constituted relations between consumer and provider (see also Chapter 4). In detailing the cross-cutting consequences of utility reform, we explore the environmental implications not of one system versus another, but of an increasingly diverse institutional landscape marked by correspondingly varied sets of consumer–provider relations.

GREEN CONSUMPTION

We begin by characterizing three ways of conceptualizing green consumption, an exercise that allows us to position our own approach and show how it differs from other models and theories.

Switching commitments

The view that the fate and future of the planet depends upon the cumulative consequences of what people do in their role as relatively autonomous shoppers is immensely pervasive. It is also a view that justifies a 'focus primarily on individual behaviour because programmes and policies aimed at reducing consumption ultimately must alter the consumption decisions made by individuals' (Brown and Cameron, 2000, p28). The idea that consumers respond to social, economic or psychological stimuli has inspired repeated rounds of research into the determinants of decision-making. If researchers could figure out just what the triggers are, policy-makers could design packages of incentives, information, signals and prompts with which to generate desired forms of behavioural change – or at least that is the hope. In following this path, commentators have been drawn into a maze of motivational psychology and economics in which consumers' actions are explained with reference to a cocktail of competing concepts such as those of altruism, status-seeking, identity, and rational calculation (Uusiatalo, 1990; Moisander, 1995). A central assumption is that green consumer practice depends upon and reflects underlying values and commitments – hence efforts to instil awareness of the global consequences of individual action.

In the UK, Powergen's Bright Sparks programme is typical. This scheme involved giving school children 'a free, low-energy lamp and a questionnaire on energy use. Families were able to buy a second lamp at the reduced price of UK£3, with £1.50 of this going to the school.' According to Powergen's promotional material: 'The project increased energy awareness among children aged between 7 and 11, saved energy and is reducing electricity bills by UK£3.1 million. Over 47,000 customers are benefiting' (Powergen, 2003).

Initiatives such as these have a number of features in common. First, and as this case illustrates rather well, the focus is on the efficiency with which services are provided. As a result, questions about changing conventions and standards of lighting simply do not arise. As in so many other situations, contemporary expectations are naturalized and normalized: they figure as non-negotiable requirements that simply have to be met. Second, such programmes are founded upon a particular model of individual choice and agency. The underlying assumption is that consumers can reduce the weight of their personal environmental 'rucksack' if they choose to do so and if they have the necessary knowledge. Last but not least, although Powergen's programme positions families as end-consumers, it tacitly acknowledges that the household infrastructure is part of the electricity network as a whole. By giving away low-energy lamps, this company is, on however small a scale, changing the demand profile and, hence, the sorts of challenges it faces as a provider.

To summarize and simplify, much environmental debate positions consumers as key 'switches' in the environmental system. Turned in one direction and the 'metabolism' of society is endangered, turned another way and it is potentially preserved (Noorman and Uiterkamp, 1998).

Influencing the environmental options on offer

Spaargaren and Van Vliet (2000, p70) argue that there is more to consumption than shopping and that environmentally committed consumers have the power and the potential to shape the range of options on offer. In this account, green consumers figure as political actors, able to vote with more than their feet in support of collective projects like those of environmental reform. The hope, here, is that there might be a tide of 'environmental innovation ... initiated by the wish of the consumer' (Spaargaren and Van Vliet, 2000, p70) and carried along by a groundswell of popular demand. Whether this, in fact, occurs or not, the key point is the recognition that consumers have a hand in shaping options as well as exercising choice between them. As Van Vliet puts it, people are not simply end-consumers entirely isolated from the production process; in reality, they too 'participate in the organization of production–consumption cycles' (Van Vliet, 2002, p53). This can take different forms. For example, Van Vliet distinguishes between situations in which consumers opt for 'green' electricity tariffs and in which they are themselves providers, owning and using photovoltaic systems and perhaps selling 'green' power back to the grid. Developing these ideas, proponents of ecological modernization claim that when prompted by consumer demand, capitalist society can be restructured around ecological goals. More than that, they believe that with new technologies and forms of organization in place, the sustainable delivery of goods and services we have come to take for granted is a real possibility.

For this to occur, policy-makers have to take a broader view of the relation between consumption and production. Spaargaren (1997, p193) consequently recommends that policy should 'not limit itself to consumer behaviour "on the market", but should also be directed at intermediary organizations and systems which can have a direct influence on changes in household consumption patterns'. For policy, the challenge is one of helping consumers find ecologically rational ways of achieving the goals of daily life and of putting their green commitments into practice. As above, the focus is on resources rather than services and, again, contemporary conventions and standards are not, in themselves, called into question.

Reproducing more and less sustainable ways of life

A third set of arguments revolves around the proposition that patterns of consumption follow from the routine accomplishment of what people take to be 'normal' ways of life. As Røpke puts it: 'consumption is woven into everyday life' (Røpke, 1999, p403) and must be analysed as such. This conceptual move shifts the focus of attention from moments of acquisition to routines of use. Just as important, it locates people as 'practitioners' rather than 'consumers'. The dynamics of practice take centre stage for the view is that different forms of consumption, some more sustainable than others, follow in the wake of changing conventions of everyday life. In this analysis, people's routines and expectations reflect shared systems of social and cultural order. Taking a strong line, Reisch (2001, p374) goes so far as to argue that 'the non-stop society forces consumers to adopt lifestyles which are unsustainable'. This is so whatever the strength of their environmental commitment.

The idea that people are obliged to consume in order to be part of society raises a host of further questions about the relation between consumption and the production and reproduction of social difference. Bourdieu (1984) and Douglas and Isherwood (1996) have, for instance, written about how the symbolic significance of specific forms of consumption evolves. Drawing upon a rather different literature, Rip and Kemp (1998) conclude that concepts of normal and ordinary practice are intimately related to trajectories of technological and institutional change. Accordingly, technological improvements in the provision and consumption of energy and water are important not (only) because of associated efficiencies, but because tools and infrastructures shape (while also being shaped by) taken-for-granted conventions, practices and ways of life (Shove et al, 1998). In other words, technological 'fixes' to environmental problems are themselves infused with concepts of sufficient and normal practice.

To generalize and, again, simplify, these ideas suggest that patterns of sustainable consumption require and depend upon the development of correspondingly sustainable socio-technical regimes. For environmental policy, the challenge is to identify critical moments or turning points at which socio-technical trajectories and the ways of life associated with them might be nudged, if not 'steered' in a different direction. In practice, this means looking for opportunities to modulate pathways of transition through considered forms of strategic intervention, and facilitating interaction between the many actors involved in configuring sectors, services and institutions. Such methods do not revolve around the 'end-consumer', nor do they imply or require explicit commitments to specifically environmental goals. The emphasis is, instead, on the socio-technical, political and historical structuring of everyday life, with all that entails for patterns of consumption.

Representations of consumers as shoppers, citizens or practitioners generate different ways of thinking about how utilities and users interact and, hence, about what is at stake in 'greening' the connections involved. The next section explores these differences in more detail.

RESOURCES, SERVICES AND INTERDEPENDENT PRACTICES

Not surprisingly, energy policy-makers and regulators are preoccupied with resources (electricity, gas, oil, etc.) and with the rate at which these are consumed. Efforts to influence consumption, whether through prices, regulation or information, reflect this resource-based approach. So, too, do more conceptual models of households as input–output systems through which resources flow (Noorman and Uiterkamp, 1998). Gatersleben and Vleck (1998, p142) define household metabolism as 'the conversion of energy, water, material goods and services into various household functions and waste products' and go on to describe a somewhat mechanical system in which 'needs', 'opportunities' and 'abilities' combine to determine levels of environmental impact. This model is one in which individual decision-making informed by higher-level societal concepts of 'need' determines resource flows through the 'system' as a whole.

In practice, and as utilities and policy-makers are beginning to realize, metaphors of engineering and flow are of little value in understanding the practicalities of consumption. There are several reasons for this. One is that although people pay for the electricity and water they use, these are not conventional commodities. What actually matters, at least to consumers, is the services that these resources make possible. In other words, people consume electricity and water in the course of engaging in an extraordinarily diverse range of practices, including bathing, laundering, heating and cooling, cooking, watching television, using a computer and so forth, each of which has a trajectory and a dynamic of its own. While energy and water bills record resource use, they tell us little if anything about the services that are thereby delivered and that are, in a sense, the real 'objects' of consumption.

If we conclude that services, not resources, should be the focus of attention, we have to re-conceptualize the relation between utilities and their users. At the very least we have to recognize that this relationship is mediated by a complex array of intervening technological systems through which consumers are, quite literally, connected to wider infrastructures of provision.

Clear-cut distinctions between consumers, on the one hand, and providers, on the other, do not adequately account for all of the intermediate institutions and socio-technical systems involved. It is, for instance, important to keep sight of the point that energy- and water-consuming devices such as night store heaters, power showers, washing machines and freezers are themselves appropriated and 'domesticated' (Lie and Sorensen, 1996) with reference to existing, but nonetheless dynamic, concepts of appropriate domestic practice. As numerous authors have observed (Strasser, 1982; Cowan, 1983; Parr, 1999), technologies, conventions and practices co-evolve. Automatic washing machines have, for instance, transformed what is involved in doing the wash and influenced the development of new concepts, standards and senses of obligation. Kaufmann (1998) writes about these silent injunctions in a way that illustrates the relation between the recurrent performance of a practice (like doing the washing) and its development as an emergent entity – that is, as a set of conventions that inform future performances and, hence, future forms of consumption.

There are other interdependencies at play in developing, sustaining and operating utility networks (Shove and Chappells, 2001; Chappells, 2003). Otnes (1998, p120), for example, describes domestic consumption as a process of 'being served by, and serving, a number of essentially collective socio-material systems'. Each time we switch on a light bulb we are connected to an invisible hinterland of expertise, wiring, utility investment and power generation. The act of flicking the switch is, in an important sense, part of this complex system. It is so because consumers and users are actively involved in reproducing and sustaining collective socio-material and related expert systems. Networks require recurrent use in order to survive – a point clearly illustrated by the demise of previously extensive systems such as those of the telegraph or of canal-based transport in the UK.

Households may not know much about what lies behind their taps and socket outlets – Garrett (1997) reports that many UK consumers are unsure exactly who their local supplier is – but they nonetheless occupy a pivotal position as the owners and managers of the sensitive 'fingertips' of the network as a whole. In recognizing this point, Patterson (2003) makes a compelling case for extending definitions of utility infrastructures to include the buildings and dwellings that are supplied with power. Though not owned by electricity or water companies, these structures and the equipment they contain are central to the operation of the system as whole. This type of interdependence is exemplified by the experiences of an electricity company operating in rural Northumbria, in the north of England. The company has been particularly successful in persuading householders to install electric night store heaters. These devices consume cheap-rate electricity during the night and give out heat during the day. From the utility's point of view, they are intended to help spread the daily pattern of demand. However, the campaign has been so effective that the company has created a new problem of its own making: the daily peak is now at 2.00 a.m. when all of the night store heaters kick in! There is little that can be done in response since the heaters are owned by householders, not by the utility, and as such have a dual existence as part of the regional electricity system and as part of people's homes.

The paragraphs above suggest that institutions and infrastructures are sustained and reproduced by and through the actions and practices of those who use them, *and* that these systems structure those same actions and practices. It is therefore important to review the relation between different systems of provision and the construction and management of demand.

SYSTEMS OF PROVISION AND THE CONSTRUCTION AND MANAGEMENT OF DEMAND

We are used to the idea that energy, water and waste management will be centrally provided by a limited number of organizations, often state monopolies. But this is not the only option.

Fine and Leopold describe and characterize the chains or systems of provision that unite 'a particular pattern of production with a particular pattern of consumption' (Fine and Leopold, 1993, p4). Services such as housing and healthcare can be provided by the state, by private companies, by oneself, or by one's family and friends. More commonly, systems of provision involve quite complex combinations of multiple modes. As we will see, competitive and collaborative relations and interactions between producers, distributors, retailers and consumers have important consequences for the long-term construction of demand and for the design and operation of energy, water and waste management systems.

The following historical examples, one from each sector, illustrate something of what is involved and provide a general introduction to themes and tensions explored in more detail in the chapters that follow.

Providing and consuming water

Water, which is essential to sustain human life, is a natural resource and not one that is manufactured or made. In talking about how water is 'provided' and 'consumed', we are, in effect, talking about how it is channelled, contained, distributed and treated, and about how access to it is managed and controlled. The move from communal or private wells to mains water supplies represents an important moment in the history of water provision. With this step, what Taylor and Trentmann (2004) refer to as the 'liquid politics' of flow acquired new meaning and character. Most obviously, categories such as those of provider and consumer make sense in a way that they did not before. In the UK, as in a number of other countries, the history is one in which multiple private water companies, initially set up to supply cities and metropolitan areas, were taken over by municipalities. In London, the 1902 Metropolitan Water Act bought out water companies and placed water provision in the hands of the Metropolitan Water Board, with local authority representation (Taylor and Trentmann, 2004, p6). During recent years, public-sector monopolies have been dismantled with the result that water is once again provided by the private sector.

These institutional transformations reflect changing understandings of what water consumption is about. During the late 1800s, water was strongly associated with public health, sanitation and civilization (Roche, 2000). The view was that people, and especially poor people, needed more water and a more reliable supply of it in order to maintain standards important for public health and essential for civilized society (Ogle, 1996; Melosi, 2000). Massive private investment in plumbing, taps, baths and showers – indeed, the invention of the bathroom as a whole – was inspired by logic of this kind. At the same time, such investment supposed and contributed to the development of relatively integrated systems of water provision and wastewater treatment. The parameters of water consumption relate to developments in water-using practices, such as regular bathing, and to the installation of mediating technologies, including toilets, taps, bathtubs and washing machines. Infrastructures such as the massive Thirlmere aqueduct that carries water from the hills of the Lake District to the city of Manchester or the water reservoirs built in the 'Brabantsche Biesbosch', The Netherlands, during the 1970s were, in turn, designed and sized to cope with anticipated patterns of demand (Chappells, 2003).

The fine details of just how water systems work – where and on what scale investments are made, and why – reflect the mixtures of public- and private-sector interests involved, and more abstract but often related concepts of water as a 'right', as a free good and as a scarce commodity. In the UK, newly privatized water companies have an uphill battle to persuade their 'customers' to limit consumption during times of drought. As rate payers, people had been willing to save water for the public good; but in their new role as consumers it was difficult to see why they should cut back to alleviate problems faced by a handful of private companies.

As this section indicates, systems of consumption and production intersect. In this case, it is clear that systems of provision, including institutional modes and physical infrastructures, have consequences for, and at the same time reflect, ideas about what water is (Strang, 2004) and about the societal, as well as personal, importance of water-consuming practices.

Providing and consuming electricity

The history of domestic electrification is, in essence, a history of inventing need. Although now an essential part of daily life, electricity was first used as a substitute for a variety of existing resources, including wood, gas, oil, wax and steam. Since heat, power and light could all be provided by other means, the system builders of electricity networks (Hughes, 1983) confronted not one but a number of related challenges in figuring out where and how to position this new 'product'. Unlike water, electricity really does have to be made, and as others have explained, the practicalities of electricity production have immediate consequences for the organization of consumption. Two features are especially important. First, and again unlike water, electricity is rather difficult to store. It is therefore important to keep supply and demand in balance. Second, it is generally more efficient to keep generators and power plants running continuously.

These production-oriented considerations exerted a powerful influence over the first efforts to construct demand. What was required was not 'demand', in general, but an evenly distributed demand profile produced as a result of the voluntary actions (connections, disconnections, and switchings on and off) of a multitude of individual consumers. In order to achieve this ideal, providers had to pick consumers carefully and influence what they did and when.

To begin with, households used electricity to replace other forms of lighting, particularly gas. This generated demand for electricity during the night, but not the day. Other uses had to be constructed and new daytime and summer loads had to be built if the system was to function effectively. Hughes (1983) and Nye (1992) have written about the deliberate configuration of domestic, industrial and transport-related demand and about the public- and private-sector interests involved. In the home, electric heaters and cookers were developed, along with vacuum cleaners, toasters, washing machines, dishwashers, potato peelers and knife grinders – all appliances through and with which to sell electricity (Forty, 1986, p87). This is not the place to describe the slow and rather erratic wiring-up of Western society. For present purposes, it is enough to notice that the potential benefits of being wired up relate to the range of electric appliances in circulation and that having a fully wired home is not in itself much value, unless one also owns an array of electrical appliances. As noted above, the acquisition, use and appropriation of things such as automatic washing machines have further consequences for what it means to wash well and, therefore, for the definition of practices and habits, many of which now 'require' appliances that, in turn, necessitate a steady and reliable supply of electrical power.

In subsequent chapters we discuss contemporary efforts to manage demand for electricity in order to reduce emissions of CO_2. We also reflect on the environmental implications of different scales of provision and, in particular, the possibilities afforded by more localized forms of power generation. In exploring these themes we keep the relation between consumption and production centre stage.

Producing and managing domestic waste

Domestic dustbins of the kind that local authorities empty on a regular basis symbolize and, in a more direct way, embody relations between the household, figuring here as the producer of waste, and the organizations involved in waste management. The very existence of these bins supposes a rather extensive infrastructure of local taxation, municipal responsibility, centralized waste planning, specialized trucks and teams of dedicated employees. Their size and form reflect further assumptions about the volume of household waste and about the frequency and method of collection. The modern 'wheelie bin' is, for example, designed to accommodate a large quantity of undifferentiated rubbish. It is also made to be picked up and emptied mechanically by a purpose-built vehicle in which the contents are crushed and carried away. While this is a scenario routinely repeated across the cities of Western Europe, such arrangements have a rather short history.

It is again a history that relates to urbanization, public health and sanitation. But there is more to it than that. For one thing, it is only recently that homes have begun to produce what counts as rubbish on any scale. In addressing this issue, authors such as Thompson (1979) O'Brien (1999) and Strasser (2000) examine the social and economic properties of waste from somewhat different perspectives. They are, however, in agreement that what counts as waste varies from one context to another, and that analysis of this category and of what it contains provides important insight into the social organization of production and consumption.

There was, for instance, a time when worn-out cotton clothing was much sought after as a raw material for paper-making. Equally, there was a time when scraps of food would have gone directly into the belly of a local pig. Whether a rag is of value or not depends upon how scraps of fabric figure in the wider economy. The volume and nature of the 'waste' that now finds its way into the bin consequently depends upon a whole sequence of judgements and evaluations applied to materials and artefacts as they travel through the value chains of society. It also depends upon the existence of alternative destinations. For example, when open fires were common, they were commonly used to incinerate all manner of unwanted materials. As a result, there was much less to put in the bin.

This is not the place to go into the history and politics of rubbish management. For now, the important point is that changing definitions of waste have implications for the boundary between public and private responsibility, and vice versa. Having said that, there is no doubt that the contemporary economic and environmental costs of managing the waste streams of today's consumer society are considerable. Environmentally inspired programmes designed to minimize the amount of rubbish dumped in landfill sites bring with them new options, categories and classifications. For example, some require households to accept and internalize new categories, to separate different types of waste and to modify routines and practices to suit. Others do not involve separation at source. As we shall see, exactly how the 'work' of waste management is distributed and managed within the home or by an increasingly complex array of public- and private-sector organizations is of some significance for the number of fractions into which rubbish is sorted (that is, for the types of rubbish produced) and for what happens to it next.

If ours is, indeed, a wasteful society, it is so for a variety of structural reasons. In arguing that categories of waste and rubbish are made and reproduced in ways that have to do with the social, political and economic ordering of society, we bring a new perspective to bear on practices such as recycling. Rather than seeing these as expressions of personal environmental commitment, we focus again on the systems of provision (including provision of waste management) involved and on the categories and classifications that these entail.

INSIGHTS AND IMPLICATIONS

In the UK, up to 10 per cent of average weekly household expenditure goes on fuel and power (King, 1997). Despite this, and despite the environmental importance of the utilities, efforts to define and analyse sustainable consumption persistently fail to conceptualize the sorts of issues involved. Contemporary theories of consumption have serious limitations when applied to such inconspicuous subjects as energy, waste and water (Shove and Warde, 2001). A recent review of literature on sustainable consumption produced for the UK's Sustainable Development Commission (Jackson and Michaelis, 2003) illustrates this point. This report aims to 'provide an overview of the extensive literatures on consumer behaviour and lifestyle change' (Jackson and Michaelis, 2003, p4). It takes stock of different accounts of 'true' and 'false' needs and examines the 'pathology' of consumerism. It highlights the symbolic role of goods and their importance for identity, for group belonging and for providing meaning in our lives. Still searching for explanations as to why we consume as we do, the authors consider the possibility that 'evolutionary forces have conditioned us to continually strive to position ourselves in relation to the opposite sex and with respect to our sexual competitors', and that consumption has become an integral part of such positioning (Jackson and Michaelis, 2003, p29).

While the report acknowledges that much everyday consumption is invisible, both to us and to our sexual competitors, it has little to say that is of value in trying to conceptualize the dynamics of energy and water consumption and waste generation. These are simply not areas in which acquisition and status run together, in which the pursuit of novelty is a driving force in its own right or in which symbolic markers and signs of social differentiation, let alone sexual competition, are much in evidence.

In this chapter, we have identified some of the distinctive features of energy and water consumption and of waste management. Unlike most other consumer goods, energy and water are important not in their own right, but for the services they make possible. In this context, an adequate theory of sustainable consumption has to account for the ways in which resource use is modulated and mediated by social practice and by the tools and technologies involved along the way. Developing this idea, we conclude that it makes better sense to concentrate not on consumption as such, but on the development, transformation and reproduction of practices, the successful accomplishment of which require the use of certain amounts of energy and water or which result in the production of certain forms of 'waste'. Although households are often only dimly aware of the resources they use, and although few know much about the social and technical infrastructures of supply, we argue that patterns of consumption are intimately related to the systems of provision involved. In contrast to literatures of the kind referred to above, we pay close attention to the relation between production and consumption and to the manner in which they are interdependent.

Although sometimes useful, the two-part language of consumption and production can also be misleading. In the following chapters we show how crucial environmental resources are filtered through multiple systems of provision and mediated by social and technical infrastructures in ways that are of defining importance for the specification and transformation of demand.

3

Infrastructural Change and Sustainable Consumption

The extent to which technologies define the practices of consumers and structure systems of provision is not immediately obvious, especially in the context of recent infrastructural fragmentation and flux. When viewed alongside the rather static, stable and undifferentiated technical networks of provision that consumers have become accustomed to, it becomes apparent that new combinations of power stations, distribution networks, landfill sites, bins, pylons, transformers, reservoirs and tanks create significantly different contexts for consumption. In this chapter, we reflect upon the changing relations between consumers and infrastructures and upon new combinations of technologies and practice currently redefining the meaning of service provision.

The role that technologies play in structuring possibilities for consumption and in defining demand has been the subject of lively debate. Technological infrastructures have been portrayed as both constraints (Bauman, 1990) as well as facilitators of everyday life and domestic consumption (Otnes, 1988). Sociologists of technology have further emphasized the part that utilities play in configuring technologies and, hence, in shaping the intensity with which resources are used (Cowan, 1983; Forty, 1986; Bijker, 1995). Although grids, conceptualized as highly integrated physical networks and nodes, can denote stability or – put negatively – inertia, they do change over time and in ways that can significantly redefine relations between utilities and users.

In this chapter, we examine the role of technologies and large technological systems in shaping consumption. This serves to show how technologies, utilities and users are jointly implicated in constructing opportunities for sustainable service provision and the management of demand. Taking concepts of consumption and demand to be the products of certain social and technical contexts, we identify five modes of utility network organization – autonomous, piecemeal, integrated, universal and marketized – each representing moments in European infrastructure management. Different modes of organization are described with reference to examples from the UK and The Netherlands to show how these create and reproduce distinctive contexts for supply-and-demand management.

Turning our attention to recent utility transformations, we reflect upon patterns of infrastructural change connected to privatization and liberalization and upon what these mean for utility and user relations and associated models of demand management. Infrastructural reorganization can take many forms. Patterns of integration and fragmentation have a powerful influence on consumer choice and demand management opportunities. As well as describing some of the processes through which grids and consumer relations are being reformed, we isolate key aspects of environmental renewal that are especially relevant to the restructuring of consumer and provider relations.

MODES OF NETWORK ORGANIZATION AND CONTEXTS FOR CONSUMPTION

In this section we briefly describe five different modes of network organization and their underlying models of demand. Each mode is illustrated with reference to particular organizational arrangements found at different moments in the development of British and Dutch networks. The modes we describe are not straightforwardly associated with moments in the chronological evolution of utility systems. Different modes can co-exist at the same time in different situations or contexts, but with varying degrees of relative significance.

Autonomous modes of organization

Before water was contained and pooled in large-scale reservoirs and made available through regional distribution networks, consumers had to draw upon local resources, including wells, rivers and lakes. Similarly, before the advent of central collection-and-disposal systems, householders had to find ways of dealing with their waste – one approach in the UK being to burn this on domestic fires and spread the resulting ash on fields or gardens. These systems represent early forms of self-management in which the role of provider and consumer is united. This mode of organization revolves around a model of demand management in which self-providers meet their own needs. Although utility networks are generally configured to provide for a much wider

29

variety of needs, there are still some households who generate their own electricity, treat their own water or compost their own waste on site.

Piecemeal modes of organization

Like the 'autonomous' mode described above, piecemeal systems are built around localized supplies. A key difference is that independent suppliers are involved in providing services to a somewhat extended customer base. Typical of this mode are the electricity systems developed by private companies and municipalities during the early 1900s in the UK and The Netherlands. These initially incorporated small generating sets designed to provide lighting services to limited numbers of commercial and domestic consumers in urban centres (Hannah, 1979; Bläser, 1992). Hughes (1983) describes how these arrangements developed within UK cities as more and more private entrepreneurs and municipal authorities constructed their own local supply grids and extended their areas of operation with little external regulation or centralized control. According to Graham and Marvin (1995), these networks can also be conceived of as 'islands', in the sense that they are small, locally based and internally focused with a high level of technical, social and economic variability between cities and regions.

While 'autonomous' modes require consumers to act as the co-managers of demand, 'piecemeal' systems shift the balance of control toward the provider. Piecemeal networks are based on the assumption that utility providers (be they private companies or municipal authorities) can meet maximum anticipated demand. This mode is underpinned by a logic that supports the building of supply capacity to meet peak demand. Methods chosen to manage demand under piecemeal arrangements reflect the specific priorities of local suppliers. This means that systems are likely to be developed and managed in rather ad hoc or uncoordinated ways that contribute to the development of a high proportion of idle 'capacity'. There are, again, contemporary parallels. For example, some local authorities now generate and distribute electricity to their tenants and build systems that run alongside the main grid (Gosling, 1996; Hodgson, 1997).

Integrated modes of organization

This mode is characterized by a more 'integrated' approach to network management in which 'spare' capacity is viewed as productive 'space' that needs to be exploited. In respect of electricity, both Forty (1986) and Hughes (1983) have argued that the concept of 'load factor' is critical in explaining the development of more integrated forms of network management. Load factor refers to the ratio of the amount of electricity supplied during a specified period to the amount of electricity it would have been possible to supply at maximum output during that period. For many electricity managers, load factor has become the key indicator of technical or commercial efficiency, a view founded on the notion that commercial and operational benefits are best achieved through regularity of load and the maximum practical utilization of generating capacity (Hughes, 1983). This has led many suppliers to consider how they might attract new loads and diversify their customer base.

Moves toward network integration are associated with economic imperatives and political priorities. For example, following World War I, the UK government contended that fragmented technical and institutional structures constrained national economic growth and social development and so set about developing a programme of regional consolidation (Hannah, 1979). An important feature of these more integrated regional arrangements was the centralized coordination and management of loads. Newly appointed load dispatchers were assigned the role of matching power station output to the demand of the population they served. Demand management activities were essentially defined in terms of achieving an acceptable load factor on the assumption that optimal efficiency meant maximizing the utilization of network capacity as a whole. We now consider modes of organization characterized by an even greater degree of centralized coordination and control.

Universal modes of organization

Graham and Marvin (1995) suggest that the consolidation of utility networks is symbiotically linked to a Fordist post-war political economy of mass production, mass distribution and mass consumption. This expansionary approach is perhaps best illustrated in the case of the UK electricity network where a post-war social and political climate of 'nation-building', coupled with an unusually harsh winter in 1947, contributed to the creation of an institutional culture in which electricity load planners and forecasters came to regard demand not as something to be differentiated, promoted or controlled, but as a non-negotiable need that had to be met. Such expansionary approaches dominated electricity (and water) management in both the UK and The Netherlands from the 1950s up to the 1970s, a period during which national and regional forecasters and planners continually revised estimates of demand growth upwards, and in which grids were incrementally extended and interconnected (Patterson, 1990; Tellegen et al, 1996). The need to cater for future demand justified the construction of an extensive network of power stations, reservoirs, overhead lines, underground cables and aqueducts. This also meant that demand had to be generated in order to sustain these systems of mass production.

Marketized modes of organization

As early as the 1940s UK government economists began to have a more influential role in the development of utility networks and markets (Hannah, 1982; Sheail, 1991; Berrie, 1992). In contrast to engineers and planners, these actors had quite different ideas about how networks might be organized and managed. Instead of building extra capacity they suggested that increasing electricity supply was not necessary for the health of the national economy or population and that, in theory, certain demands could be managed or curbed without any detrimental effects. Subsequent decades have seen a burgeoning interest in the economics of the demand side. The privatization of public service monopolies across the UK and The Netherlands reflects just such a marketized approach. The associated restructuring of generation, distribution and supply networks has inevitably had a significant influence on how demand is coordinated and managed nationally and regionally. Guy et al (1997) suggest that privatized utilities have developed a closer interest in the operational efficiency of their networks and in the differentiated demands of their consumers. In essence, demand is viewed not in terms of aggregated needs that have to be met by extending network capacity. Instead, demand is understood as a complex of highly differentiated loads that can be managed or manipulated through market mechanisms.

In autonomous modes of organization, consumers themselves are responsible for defining service expectations and for deciding how resources might be allocated to meet needs. In 'piecemeal' arrangements, local suppliers are guided by the political, economic and geographical feasibility of connecting customers to networks in their designated 'patches'. Universal and integrated modes of network organization and operation are defined more by the social and political priorities of commercial companies, national and regional governments and regulators.

Infrastructural arrangements associated with each mode of organization determine where the boundaries between consumers and producers lie. Autonomous modes consist of stand-alone grids, with

Table 3.1 Modes of organization and contexts for consumption

Mode of organization	Autonomous	Piecemeal	Integrated	Universal	Marketed
Representation of consumer–provider roles	Co-providers of highly localized resources	Customers and suppliers of newly created services	Consumers and promoters of diversified demand	Passive beneficiaries and public providers of uniform services	Purchasers and promoters of differentiated products and services
Supporting infrastructural arrangements	Stand-alone self-managed grids at local scale	Patchwork of local grids providing unregulated and non-standardized services	Semi-integrated grids connecting 'compatible' loads at local and regional scale	Highly integrated national and regional 'super grids' delivering uniform resources	Partially fragmented grids matching the socially and economically defined needs of diverse utilities and users
Representation of consumption	Personal and collective need to be negotiated and managed in-house	Customer defined need to be met	Diverse needs to be nurtured, coordinated and combined	Universal and non-negotiable need to be met	Highly negotiable needs to be manipulated and managed
Model of demand management	Responsive and reflexive	Manufacture and meet	Diversify and develop	Predict and provide	Monitor and manipulate

households involved in the allocation of locally available resources as and when required. By contrast, universal networks now built around extensive, even international, 'super grids' are designed to meet extreme peaks and are built on the assumption that consumers' needs are there to be met.

Each mode revolves around a distinctive representation of consumers' roles in provision and in managing demand. Consumers sometimes figure as competent self-managers of mini-networks, and sometimes as passive customers whose non-negotiable needs must be met by public institutions and infrastructures. Alternatively, they might be positioned as rational economic actors with specific service requirements. Demand is variously regarded as something to be nurtured and manufactured, to be curbed and controlled, to be manipulated and managed or to be met at all costs. In short, Table 3.1 suggests that consumer roles and demand are social and technical constructs in so far as they reflect the priorities of different constellations of actors operating in divergent political and institutional contexts.

In isolating these modes of organization and what they mean for consumption and demand management we also make the point that multiple possibilities for the sustainable reconfiguration of networks co-exist. Even so, some modes support methods of managing demand that obviate the need for others. In this sense certain consumer or demand cultures can become 'locked in', guiding network development along certain paths and preventing the switch to alternative management regimes. For example, the universalizing post-war culture of electricity organization in the UK supported the building of more and more capacity and its interconnection through the national grid. This effectively limited opportunities for other forms of demand management.

So far, we have provided a static analysis of different types of infrastructural arrangement. In the following sections we explore ways of conceptualizing socio-technical change and the relation between different modes of organization.

UNDERSTANDING INFRASTRUCTURAL CHANGE AND TRANSITION

Hughes (1983) argues that manufacturers, utilities and regulating bodies all have vested interests in the growth and durability of particular systems. As large technical systems develop, key actors form alliances and act to protect or promote their own system against competition from others. As a consequence, technological systems reinforce themselves internally by becoming increasingly standardized and gathering 'momentum' (Hughes, 1983) or dynamic inertia (Joerges, 1988). From this perspective, technical systems not only embody the ideals, values or technological frames of the context in which they evolve, but also develop a dynamic of their own. For example, Hughes (1983) describes how the concept of 'universal' electricity supply gathered momentum during the 1890s as a supportive culture and context developed, and has since evolved into a 'super-system' with mass movement and direction.

The concept of technological 'momentum' is useful in understanding the capacity of current actors to reconfigure technologies and so implant new social and environmental contexts for the management of demand. Arguments about the momentum of technologies and technological systems are also relevant in thinking about how today's consumers might become locked into certain ways of thinking about demand and into certain modes of demand management. For example, the idea that 'demand' is something that simply has to be met has clearly influenced the options available to consumers until recently. This has implications for how conceptualizations of demand as something to be curbed or contained might be ingrained or embedded within new systems of utility management.

On the other hand, large technological systems are not closed to reinterpretation and their direction is not always irreversible. The relationship between embedded infrastructural arrangements and organizational change has been extensively analysed in the literature on innovation (David, 1985; Arthur, 1989; Berkhout, 2002).

Proponents of 'technological transition management' view infrastructural change as a multidimensional process that takes place across a number of 'levels' (Kemp et al, 1998; Geels and Kemp, 2000; Elzen et al, 2004). The basic idea is that innovations take root in relatively protected 'niches'. As they become established, so they change the configuration of the 'regime' into which (and within which) they emerge. The development of alternative technologies (for example, solar panels for electricity generation, rain water devices to collect and store water for household purposes and composting bins for domestic waste treatment) is potentially important for the continuity and/or transformation of entire socio-technological regimes (De Laat, 1996). For instance, the introduction of water-saving technologies such as vacuum toilets might require changes in consumers' routines and habits. Such a development also implies meso- or macro-level change in so far as the producers of conventional toilets and managers of sewerage systems have to find ways of accommodating new technologies and practices within existing networks.

Theories of 'transition' offer a useful way of conceptualizing change on multiple levels and of representing infrastructure system development as a process through which actors continually adapt to, and learn from, new situations (Rotmans et al, 2001). Such multi-level models of change show that there are a variety of routes possible, each moving at different speeds and each exhibiting different degrees of path dependency, lock-in and irreversibility.

Although transition theories provide useful models of sustainable transformation in utility systems, the narratives of change they offer require further scrutiny at the empirical level. The development of 'greener' networks is not always initiated by 'niche' projects, or by small-scale 'bottom-up' developments. In some situations radical changes in the organization of infrastructure networks have been initiated by the promotion of technologies by 'mainstream' actors operating at a large-scale. The introduction of mobile phones and their impact on communication networks is a classic example. The introduction and promotion of air conditioners by utilities and manufacturers and their impacts on indoor climate systems and electricity networks is another (Cooper, 1998). Clearly, there are some technological developments that do not follow the idealized 'S-curve' as implied in transition management. More important for our purposes is the point that consumers' roles in initiating technological transitions across micro, meso and macro levels are not elaborated. These require further empirical investigation.

It is clear from the above that provision and consumption are being restructured from 'niche' through to 'landscape'. Those who restrict themselves to studying the role of the end-consumer only will consequently fail to capture or comprehend the sorts of transformations currently underway. What is required and what this book aims to provide is a multilayered analysis of consumer involvement in sustainable transition through systems of energy, water and waste provision.

INFRASTRUCTURAL DYNAMICS AND NEW CONTEXTS FOR CONSUMPTION

Over the last decade there have been considerable organizational changes in the utility sectors, connected to the privatization programme, market liberalization and environmental modernization that all mark a redefinition of consumer roles in utility provision (Spaargaren, 1997; Spaargaren and Van Vliet, 2000; Graham and Marvin, 2001). Graham and Marvin (2001) argue that changing commercial, social and environmental pressures have supported the institutional and technical 'unbundling' of infrastructure networks. The concept of 'unbundling' relates to a number of dimensions of institutional and technical change – for example, the fragmentation of physical networks and setting up of new micro-grids; the separation of generation, distribution or supply activities that were previously operated by the same utility company; or the segmentation of networks by market, territory or service category. They further suggest that infrastructures have been 'virtually' segmented – as in situations where competitive service regimes and new operating rules are superimposed over existing organizational structures.

Processes of infrastructure unbundling as described by Graham and Marvin (2001) are expected to reshape the landscape of utility provision, transforming relations between network users and providers and so creating differentiated contexts for environmental and social action. Graham and Marvin (2001) claim that unbundling does not involve the replacement of old modes of organization with new ones. Instead, they describe the development of co-existing pathways operating at different spatial scales and moving at a range of speeds across different utility sectors. These pathways vary in terms of how far they embody different private, public or informal concepts of provision.

In respect of macro-level transformations in the UK and The Netherlands, the pattern is, indeed, one of multiple pathways and directions. In both countries electricity companies have been privatized and markets opened up to competition. Domestic consumers can now choose between service providers and products. The 'de-municipalization' of waste management in both countries has seen waste collection and disposal taken over by private-sector waste management companies. Municipal waste managers now bid for service contracts alongside private-sector competitors with day-to-day operations carried out by a wide spectrum of organizations, including public, private and non-profit organizations (Gandy, 1994). This picture is further complicated by the increasing popularity of home composting and recycling, with some households managing parts of their own waste cycles. While macro transformations in the Dutch and British electricity and waste sectors have followed similar trajectories, water supply routes have diverged. Water companies in the UK have been privatized since 1989. In The Netherlands, after much debate, proposals for privatization have been rejected (Tweede Kamer, 1999; Eerste Kamer, 2003). However, in both countries water supply organizations have been encouraged to develop public- and private-sector alliances in order to improve economic and environmental efficiency (NRA, 1994; Vewin, 2001).

Although the general trend is assumed to be one of a shift from a 'universal' mode of provision, the reality is a more complex situation in which private and public priorities coexist and in which networks are *both* converging globally and fragmenting locally. For the purposes of analysis, the elements and dimensions of restructuring need to be further broken down if their implications for engendering new contexts for sustainable consumption are to be understood. In the following sections we identify principal forms of network reorganization that are contributing to the greening of grids and service regimes at different levels and scales across Europe. We further reflect upon how these new network arrangements are likely to shape the capacities of different utilities and users in a variety of contexts and situations to act as the environmental managers of networks.

Differentiation of services

Increased competition in utility markets is associated with the introduction of new opportunities for the specialization and customization of utility services. Multiple providers (including local authorities, housing associations and energy service companies) can now serve customers traditionally bound to the services provided by monopoly utility companies. These new arrangements offer possibilities for consumers to choose between service providers and the packages of products or tariffs they offer. Some new service providers might have a real interest in promoting greener services – for example, where they hope to initiate niche markets for environmental goods or services or where access to localized resources is limited and efficiencies can be achieved by minimizing rather than meeting demand (Guy and Marvin, 1996). What is not clear is how the new service possibilities being created and promoted will reframe the contexts within which different types of consumers can and cannot make environmental choices.

Fragmentation of grids

In other cases the environmental renewal of networks is being facilitated through the construction of mini- or micro-grids. Analyses of infrastructural change suggest that the development of more flexible and decentralized technologies and the introduction of competition offer opportunities to develop multiple scales of organization so that consumers can become the local providers of some of their own service needs (von Meier, 1994; Moss, 2000; Van Vliet, 2002). It is argued, for instance, that low-cost and higher-efficiency decentralized technologies, such as combined heat and power or solar energy units, have created opportunities for more flexible production regimes that better match supply to demand (Künneke, 1999; Awerbuch, 2003). Arguments about the environmental benefits of 'bottom-up' or 'top-down' modes of provision or 'soft' and 'hard' paths of network development are now well rehearsed (Schumacher, 1973; Lovins, 1977; Patterson, 1990). A question that has only been partially addressed is how new, multiply configured scales of organization create diverse contexts for the sustainable management of electricity, water and waste by domestic consumers.

Autonomous systems of technology and practice

The extent to which new 'eco-home' developments allow consumers to achieve 'autonomy' from centralized technical and institutional arrangements varies widely (Barton, 1998). The initiators of many sustainable housing projects believe that it is impossible to be properly 'environmental' without some such detachment. Technologically, this is likely to involve installing renewable generation units or recycling a certain amount of water and/or waste. In practice, such initiatives are of social and symbolic as well as material significance. In exploring these arrangements we focus on the ways in which new modes of provision challenge service regimes and mainstream approaches to demand management.

New models of demand management

Privatization and the elevation of environmental concerns have prompted interest in more integrated approaches to supply-and-demand management. Whereas utility network management has previously been defined by meeting demand through supply-side investment, new arrangements have signalled a renewed interest in the efficiency of utility systems through production, distribution, supply, use and disposal. In particular, privatization has signalled the emergence of demand-side management (DSM) – an approach in which utility managers seek to engage users as the co-managers of demand (Gellings, 1996). Fundamental to the emergence of DSM has been the development of a regulatory framework that challenges engineering-based approaches to utility planning and supply management and reintroduces questions of environmental quality and economic efficiency. The extent to which these modes of network management incorporate different consumer and provider concepts of efficiency, security or reliability remains to be seen.

Table 3.2 summarizes these four types of utility-related environmental renewal, the forms of socio-technical change they imply and what this is likely to mean for the reconstruction of consumer roles in provision. Cases of environmental innovation associated with each type of infrastructural renewal are also noted.

The four themes of service differentiation, fragmentation of scales, socio-technical autonomy and demand-side management capture the principal processes through which utility and user responsibilities for sustainable provision are being defined and realized. These generic themes can be used to understand environmentally induced socio-technical change with respect to all of the resources and systems with which we deal.

Taking each in turn, Chapter 4 considers how environmentally inspired options for service differentiation – including the introduction of green tariffs and the promotion of recycling schemes – reflect the capacities of consumers and providers to generate, promote and construct new service expectations and needs. The cases of environmental renewal reviewed in Chapter 5 show how meanings of efficiency and optimal performance differ with scale. Chapter 6 considers the range of technologies and practices adopted by households who have deliberately sought to limit their dependence upon mainstream systems of provision. Finally, Chapter 7 focuses on recent efforts by water, electricity and waste utilities to enrol consumers as the co-managers of demand.

In focusing on the four aspects of environmental renewal highlighted in Table 3.2, we draw out details about the sustainable transformation of networks at micro, meso and macro levels of organization and through multiple modes and scales of provision. We further show how the dynamics and directions of infrastructural change relate to the interfacing of old and new constellations of institutional rules and technological structures.

Table 3.2 *Types of environmental renewal in utility systems*

Themes	Service differentiation	Scales of provision	Autonomous networks	Demand-side management
Processes and implications of socio-technical change	Multiple products and services and improved choice	Increased technical and institutional fragmentation and new modes of access	Mainstream disconnection and local reintegration of technologies and practices	Reconnection of supply-demand management and improved efficiency
Roles of consumers	Co-constructers of service options and choices	Co-producers of renewable resources	Initiators and self-managers of new grids and service regimes	Co-managers of systems of provision
Illustrative cases	Green electricity Waste recycling Grey water	Photovoltaic cells Local water systems Composting	Eco-homes	Storage systems Efficiency devices

4

Differentiation and Choice in Water, Electricity and Waste Services

The liberalization and deregulation of markets has facilitated the entry of many new provider organizations and service options in the electricity, water and waste sectors. The result is a new phenomenon in traditional utility–user relations: consumer choice. With respect to this, the most eye-catching form of differentiation is the development of various kinds of 'green electricity' schemes offering variable tariffs for 'green' and 'normal' electricity by traditional and newly established energy companies. Brands now on offer in The Netherlands and the UK include Natuurstroom (Nature Power) in The Netherlands and Green-Plan in the UK.

Product and service differentiation is not restricted to electricity supply. Debates on (ground)water scarcity and the desiccation of natural reserves have triggered a number of experiments in the local generation and distribution of 'household water' in The Netherlands, as well as the installation of rainwater tanks and wastewater recycling technologies in experimental sustainable housing projects both in The Netherlands and the UK. In these situations, the paradigm of 'one water quality for all household practices' is currently being challenged and waters of different qualities are being introduced.

Turning to waste, the last two decades have seen a shift from centralized collection and treatment (landfill, incineration) to various modes of waste separation at source. Domestic waste management might now involve the utilization of multiple bins and routes for the recycling, reuse and treatment of different waste streams.

This chapter examines the notion of 'differentiation' in utility sectors and what this implies for consumer roles in water, electricity and waste management. We question whether new forms of differentiation now being promoted offer providers and consumers an improved 'choice' of greener service options.

In the first section, we explore and categorize four possible types of differentiation in utility systems. In talking about differentiation, we refer not only to a greater selection of products or tariffs, but also to the new consumer and provider roles associated with novel forms of provision. We show how new types of differentiation constitute a landscape of provision quite unlike that associated with nationalized or Fordist systems of utility organization.

Our analysis of differentiated utility services allows us to identify four ideal-type consumer roles with respect to utility providers. Subsequent sections explore each of these ideal types in greater depth. These arrangements are illustrated with reference to case studies on innovation in water, waste and electricity sectors.[1] The concluding section examines what new configurations of consumer–provider relations imply for consumer choice in differentiating utility markets.

FORMS OF DIFFERENTIATION IN UTILITY SYSTEMS

In its most basic formulation, a system of utility provision can be represented as a large technological system linking natural resources, providers and consumers (see Figure 4.1).

The horizontal spine in Figure 4.1 shows the relations between consumers (C), providers (P) and resources (R). Providers are the intermediaries between consumers and natural resources, a relationship that took shape during the early stages of urbanization when consumers' direct access to resources (water extraction sites, woodlands) was replaced by mediated access sites via reservoirs, power stations or landfills. Collective socio-material systems were developed to facilitate

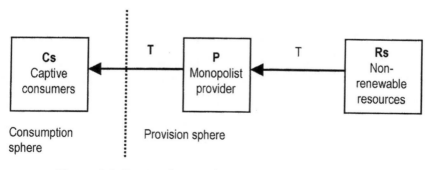

Figure 4.1 *Basic scheme of utility system of provision*

the provision of resources to consumers: these include the electricity grid, water works and waste collection and treatment schemes.

Located within these utility systems are a series of mediating technologies (Ts), including distribution, storage, efficiency and monitoring devices. Different combinations of these devices assist providers or consumers in managing resource flows in time and space. Without mediating technologies such as transformers, terminals, power stations or transport cables, electricity cannot be consumed at all.

The role of consumers in this simple representation of provision is a rather passive (or isolated/disconnected) one: there is hardly any consumer influence upon which energy, water and waste services are provided or how these are delivered, not provided. Technologies – for example, the meter in the case of water and electricity or the household bin in the case of waste – might act as a physical divide between the spheres of consumption and provision. For waste management the scheme works in a slightly different way than for water and electricity. Here 'resources' refers to treatment facilities (for example, landfills) and the 'material flow' goes in a reverse direction (from consumers to providers). However, the provision of waste 'services' starts at treatment facilities ('resources') such as incinerators, landfills or composting plants (the character of which determine the rest of the waste management chain) and moves via waste collection ('providers' such as municipalities or waste companies) to end-users of the combined waste management services.

Deregulation and liberalization, along with many other developments in utility services, have triggered the following four forms of differentiation:

1   differentiation of resource use;
2   differentiation of providers;
3   differentiation of mediating technologies; and
4   differentiation of consumer roles.

Differentiation of resource use

First of all, there has been differentiation in the resources from which electricity is generated or water is abstracted. Of course, electricity generation and water abstraction have never depended upon single sources of supply. Since the first energy crisis during the 1970s, the energy sector has become less dependent upon crude oil from the Middle East and has increasingly utilized a variety of resources – including North Sea oil, uranium, gas and hydropower (Ministry of Economic Affairs, 1995). The substitution of fossil fuels by more renewable resources implies further differentiation, including the development and exploitation of biomass, solar and wind resources.

Likewise, there have always been various sources for the abstraction of water – for example, groundwater, surface water or well water. Opportunities for water abstraction are increasingly limited, either physically or through regulation, due to desiccation of natural reserves (Van Vliet, 1995). Since the 1990s, water companies have sought alternative sources and treatment methods to fulfil the growing need for drinking water. New treatment techniques such as infiltration of surface water in riverbanks and membrane filtration have opened abstraction routes for otherwise unusable water resources.

In the case of waste, resource differentiation relates to new methods of final treatment or disposal. In terms of waste treatment, landfill sites have now been supplemented by incineration and composting sites for domestic waste, as well as by centrally managed reuse or recycling of glass, cans and paper.

The differentiation of resources is not necessarily indicative of changing relations between providers and consumers. The changes we have described can all be introduced in a regime in which captive consumers are supplied by monopolistic providers (see Figure 4.2).

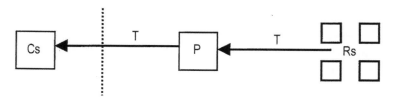

Figure 4.2 *Utility system of provision: Differentiated resources*

Differentiation of providers

The abolition of monopolistic modes of provision means that many new providers can enter utility markets, and develop and promote new niche products, systems and services. New providers may be organized quite differently from traditional utilities. Some are only trading organizations that act as intermediaries between electricity producers and household consumers (such as the internet-based Green Choice in The Netherlands). Consumer associations, environmental non-governmental organizations (NGOs), windmill co-operatives and single consumers may also act as providers of utility services.

Figure 4.3 shows the differentiation of providers. Various providers make use of the same distribution network to which consumers are connected.

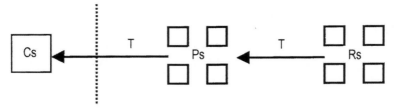

Figure 4.3 *Utility system of provision: Differentiated providers*

Differentiation of mediating technologies

Technologies for distribution of electricity and water or for the collection of waste are also being reconfigured, as are those used to monitor consumption and user access to electricity and water networks. Many technologies, like local distribution networks, sanitary systems, meters, taps, sockets and bins were developed in the course of establishing nationalized networks. Forms of institutional and environmental renewal mean that such technologies may be replaced by a new range of devices – for example, combined heat-and-power (CHP) generators, rainwater toilets, 'smart' meters, solar panels or duo-bins.

Figure 4.4 illustrates a scenario in which there is a differentiation of providers and of ways in which electricity, water and waste services are distributed, stored or monitored. Intermediate technologies in this arrangement might include advanced digital meter systems for self-monitoring of resource use and/or enabling tariff differentiation, or in-house storage devices for rainwater. Many of these technologies enable or even require the transfer of former provider responsibilities (that is, water or electricity generation, storage, monitoring and sorting of waste) to – or at least towards – consumers, a move which, in effect, 'softens' the divide between spheres of consumption and provision.

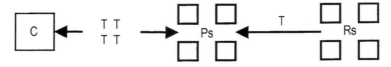

Figure 4.4 *Utility system of provision: Differentiated intermediate technologies*

Differentiation of consumer roles

Figure 4.4 provides an almost complete representation of utility system differentiation – encompassing multiple resources, diverse providers and mediating technologies. Yet, it fails to tell us much about one essential aspect: that of the differentiation of consumer roles vis-à-vis providers. This missing element is added to our representation of utility system differentiation in Figure 4.5.

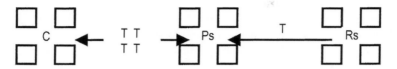

Figure 4.5 *Utility system of provision: Differentiated consumer roles*

The consumption of electricity, water or waste services is generally 'inconspicuous' (Shove, 1997). There are, of course, elaborate forms of garden lighting, luxury bathrooms or giant fridges that may flag up one's hedonistic lifestyle; but making distinction through the consumption of utility services is still awkward compared to more conspicuous activities such as car driving or wearing fashionable clothing. The fragmentation of utility markets and possibilities for greater differentiation of goods and services provide an opportunity for utility consumption to become increasingly conspicuous through the symbolic potential associated with differentiated systems of provision (Southerton, 2000). The extent to which processes of lifestyle differentiation can be attributed to the differentiation of systems of utility provision is not yet clear. However, it is possible to identify a number of ways in which consumer roles are being redefined in accordance with the types of utility differentiation identified above. The four ideal-typical scenarios sketched in Figure 4.6 define the conditions for a new range of possible consumer roles with respect to providers. The first type of consumer role – captive consumer – offers the least possibilities for social or environmental distinction, whereas the last one – co-provider – offers consumers an extended range of opportunities for developing different forms of utility provision and for creating new lifestyle options.

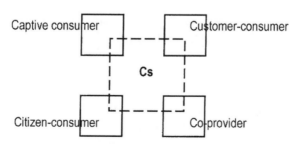

Figure 4.6 *Differentiated consumer roles*

Captive consumers

This role is normally associated with monopolistic modes of provision. The traditional relationship between utility providers and clients is that of a single regional supplier serving captive consumers who have no chance to choose between providers, products or services. As utility services are rather uniform, conspicuous consumption and social distinction by means of electricity and water consumption – let alone waste disposal – are not likely to occur. Market differentiation signals the end of captive consumption per se. Although it might be possible to choose between providers, switching supplier can be difficult due to high transaction costs, obligations to use provider-specific meters or because information on tariffs and conditions is far from transparent (see, for instance, the account Summerton (2004) provides regarding the situation in California). In effect, end-users may still feel that they are captive consumers of a utility company that continues to dominate the regional market.

Customers

Through the process of liberalization, providers redefine their roles: no longer the suppliers of uniform services to captive consumers, many now see themselves as delivering a range of services to a differentiated market of customers and clients. Suddenly, the needs and preferences of customers matter to providers. Their interest is in developing new products and services and in strengthening customer relations. Service providers also have a stake in keeping certain groups of customers satisfied – after all, consumers now have some choice between competing providers and services.

Citizen-consumers

Some providers appeal to their customers not only as consumers, but also as environmentally conscious citizens whose actions are informed by social or environmental goals. There has been product differentiation for the sake of the environment, the developing world or other societal goals for some decades now: fair-trade coffee (fair prices for small coffee farmers), 'clean' clothes (no child labour involved) and Forest Stewardship Council (FSC) timber (products from sustainably managed tropical forest) are well-known examples. In terms of utility services, linking service provision to societal goals and asking consumers to pay extra for the privilege is quite new. Green electricity schemes are designed to persuade consumers to contribute to the greening of energy production as a whole. The idea here is that responsibility for the environmental modernization of electricity production is partly transferred from the state and energy companies to the end-users of electricity. Instead of being anonymous end-users, electricity consumers are appealed to as moral or ethical actors.

Co-providers

In addition to situations in which water, electricity and waste services flow from providers to consumers, new technological and institutional opportunities enable consumers to generate these services on their own. Such arrangements are sometimes initiated by citizen-consumers – for instance, those who wish to disconnect or to be independent of large technical systems. In other cases, providers take the initiative to decentralize generation or treatment facilities for one reason or another. As a result, some new form of consumer involvement is required. Figure 4.7 illustrates the co-provision option, in which consumers exploit resources directly as well as benefiting from the grid-based provision of water, electricity or waste services.

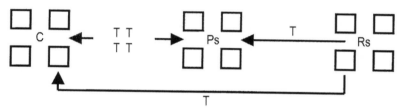

Figure 4.7 *Utility system of provision: Co-provision*

A number of examples of co-provision can be mentioned here: consumers with solar panels on their homes provide some of their own energy services, as do owners of rainwater systems for water or home composters. Co-provision may also take the form of collective provision: as a member of a local windmill association, consumers participate in the provision of green electricity to the grid.

The four types of consumer roles we have identified are associated with contrasting forms of differentiation in utility systems of provision. In the following section we use the four categories of captive, customer, citizen-consumer and co-provider to evaluate cases of 'green' differentiation in water, electricity and waste systems in the UK and The Netherlands. In each of the cases that we review, we assess the extent to which these arrangements facilitate the environmental reform of systems of provision.

CAPTIVE CONSUMERS IN DIFFERENTIATED UTILITY MARKETS

Although liberalization aims to introduce consumer choice, in reality not all consumers are in a position to respond. To illustrate this we discuss consumer roles in relation to experiments with different qualities of water.

Since the early 1970s, when water saving became an issue in The Netherlands, dual water systems have been proposed as a way of conserving treated drinking water. Debates have focused on how to provide a supply of lower quality water for uses such as toilet flushing, cleaning and gardening. Dutch water companies and national policy-makers often rejected the idea for various reasons (*Installatie, 1985* Ministry of Environment, 1993; Van Vliet, 1995). These arguments are summarized in a public information booklet produced by the Dutch Ministry of Environment (1994, p29, our translation):

> Every now and then it is proposed to use other kinds of water (of minor quality) in households – for instance, to flush the toilet. The double pipes and double connections needed for this alternative make it, however, very expensive. Besides, the chance of misconnection between pipes will increase, implying an extra risk for public health. In general, individual use of grey water and rainwater is a vulnerable and costly process. The cost-effectiveness of such homebound systems is so low that it is better to spend the money on other, more urgent environmental problems.

Until recently, one of the leading principles of national policy for domestic water supply is that only one quality of water should be supplied for human consumption in all households (Ministry of Environment, 1993). This principle is designed to protect citizens and prevent them from consuming unsafe or unhealthy water. Many utilities and policy-makers contend that a dual water system would introduce a risk of contamination between the two systems, resulting in polluted drinking water.

Nonetheless, since 1995 there have been several new experiments with so-called household water systems. These have taken place in typical 'niche-market' environments. Household water projects generally consist of additional supply systems next to drinking water supply that distribute treated rainwater or surface water from the direct neighbourhood of the residential sites. This second water system is generally meant for toilet flushing, washing laundry and gardening.

The emergence of household water projects can partly be explained by structural changes in the drinking water sector itself. All Dutch water companies currently hold a 'natural monopoly' in the region they serve, especially in the domestic consumption market, but face increasing pressure to reduce production costs, as well as to reduce water abstraction from groundwater resources. These pressures are encouraging them to renew their policies and develop a more client-oriented, market-based approach (see Stoter, 1994; interview WMO, 1999, and interview Nuon, 1998). Instead of simply issuing water bills, providers are increasingly inclined to listen to the wishes of consumers and municipalities (interview WMO, 1999). Municipalities that are planning major residential areas have taken new approaches to water management and have asked water companies to cooperate in new housing projects such as Leidsche Rijn and IJburg (interview GWL, 1999). This kind of collaborative planning has resulted in a number of experiments. Some are small scale (for example, 200 houses in Wageningen); others are larger (18,000 homes in IJburg); some involve using water from local ditches and canals (Wageningen); whereas others rely on half-treated surface water tapped from a major transport pipe (Leidsche Rijn).

By 1999 there were six new residential sites in which a novel household water system had been installed and which had been given 'experimental' status by the Ministry of Environment. This means that the projects are closely monitored for their environmental, social and health aspects in order to provide an input to future policy decisions on water supply. Although very different in terms of size and resource base, the systems have in common the feature that they all provide water of less than drinking quality through a second piped system that is connected to toilets, washing machines and the outdoor tap.

Since the initiation of the first household water projects in The Netherlands, there has been lively debate regarding the net environmental benefits and the costs of household water systems. A preliminary outcome has been that each household water system must be evaluated in terms of its positive or negative impacts on the environment, as well as in relation to economic costs. These evaluations are highly dependent upon the location of the scheme and the source for the drinking water that is distributed (Van den Burg et al, 1999).

Although many water companies have suggested that household water projects are partly motivated by the 'wish of our customers' (see Vaessen, 1998, among others), studies of public acceptance of household water systems have only been executed after household water systems have been put into operation. Monitoring surveys conducted soon after the new systems were installed revealed only a few problems of acceptance and adaptation. In Leidsche Rijn (Utrecht), consumers reportedly experienced no difference in the cleanliness of laundry washed with household water, and had no problems using lower quality water to flush toilets (*Utrechts Nieuwsblad*, 2000).

A social monitoring study in Wageningen (Van Vliet, 2000) revealed that during the experiment, users learned more about their own water consumption and about environmental problems related to water consumption in general. A large majority were happy to have the system installed. However, some respondents noted that they would have liked to have participated in decisions about the design of the project and specification of the systems. Some residents complained that the information they received in advance was inadequate, especially since a large proportion of users only found out about the experimental system after moving in to their new homes.

In general, household water systems have received a mixed response from consumers. However, all household water experiments came to an end in 2003 after an evaluation by the Ministry of Environment. The environmental benefits of household water projects compared to single water supply were not as large as expected, although this differed from project to project. Moreover, the dual systems appeared to be quite expensive in comparison with conventional single-water supply systems. However, it was the risk to health that was the decisive factor leading to the cancellation of the projects. Due to misconnection between the drinking-water supply system and the pipes of the household water system in two experiments, people were drinking lower quality household water for quite some time while flushing their toilets with high quality drinking water. The ministry concluded that the supply of household water by water companies through large-scale dual pipeline systems should no longer be allowed (Tweede Kamer, 2003). Proposals for smaller-scale individual systems are still considered.

Evaluation

Although household water systems involve the extensive reconfiguration of technical infrastructures, the way in which such systems were introduced and communicated to residents in the Dutch schemes described above was not especially innovative. The decision to build a dual network was made by the water companies and the municipalities, and there was no consumer involvement in specifying the design or layout of household systems or in specifying possible uses of household water. Many new residents only found out about the system after they bought the house. In these schemes differentiation in water provision had nothing to do with consumer choice. The implementation of the household water systems we have described therefore fits into our category of 'captive-consumer' as shown in Figure 4.2.

CUSTOMERS IN DIFFERENTIATED UTILITY MARKETS

While the previous section shows that consumers can still be 'captive', even in differentiated utility markets, there are cases in which liberalization has changed the utility companies' attitudes toward their consumers. In most advertisements and promotional literature, utilities now often address consumers as 'customers' rather than anonymous end-users. What the role of 'customer' really means in utility markets varies from case to case. Here we illustrate some newly constructed 'customer' roles in electricity provision and water supply.

The electricity sectors of The Netherlands and the UK serve as an example of how uniform public utilities have become fragmented after the gradual liberalization of electricity markets. Network management, electricity production and distribution have been de-coupled and privatized. Distribution companies are now competing for large clients, as well as for household consumers. As the basic product (electricity) is the same, competition is promoted through the differentiation of multiple services associated with electricity supply. Utilities' attempts to promote differentiation with respect to the sources of electricity supply are especially interesting for our purposes.

Although electrons are always the same, energy companies have succeeded in selling different kinds of electricity to different clients. Green electricity schemes are the result of product differentiation designed to meet the 'needs' of consumers willing to pay more for electricity generated by renewable resources, such as wind, sun, hydropower or biomass. Since small non-utility providers now have access to national or regional grids, they can develop and promote their own brands of 'green' electricity. New service providers range from small windmill co-operatives delivering as much electricity to the grid as their members can consume (such as Meerwind in The Netherlands; www.meerwind.nl), to intermediate organizations which buy green electricity from large and small generators and distribute it to clients all over the country. Some provider organizations do not have any direct involvement in the maintenance of grids, windmills or power plants but simply act as trading bodies. Many of these companies compete with conventional energy suppliers, but claim to provide a purer form of 'green' electricity than their mainstream rivals (for example, Greenchoice and Echte Energie in The Netherlands).

A number of UK electricity companies have developed renewable sources of energy, and some have recognized that niche markets exist where customers are willing to switch to green electricity or to fund investment in green electricity generation. For instance, the energy company Powergen invites consumers to switch to their 'GreenPlan', which promises to match 'every unit of electricity supplied to GreenPlan customers with one from a renewable source'. The chosen source is hydroelectric power. Every unit of electricity used is also matched by a contribution from Powergen to a so-called GreenPlan fund, which supports renewable energy technology development (www.powergen.co.uk).

With the opening of the Dutch electricity market for household consumers (July 2001 for green electricity, July 2004 for all electricity), old and new providers have invested in advertising. For the first time consumers are being asked to consider switching to another electricity provider on the basis that they are 'greener', cheaper or more service oriented than their competitors. The possibility for domestic consumers to select between different providers, or between types of resources and service packages, signals the end of their role as captive consumers and the start of a new identity as a 'customer'. Yet, it is questionable whether all customers take this possibility seriously. With the opening of the Dutch green electricity market in 2001, many providers expected consumers to switch to green electricity because energy tax exemptions made green electricity tariffs equal to those of normal electricity. Now that the whole market has been opened up to competition, the government has decided not to subsidize consumers of green electricity anymore by tax exemptions on green electricity supply. The rationale behind such tax exemptions was that they would stimulate not only consumption of green electricity, but also the domestic production of it. Over the years, it became clear that the second goal was not reached at all. Instead of building wind turbines, utilities have primarily imported green electricity from neighbouring countries and sold it free of environmental taxes to their customers. Therefore, it was decided to stimulate domestic production of green electricity by another means: specifically by subsidizing investments in green electricity production capacity (Tweede Kamer, 2004).

There is some evidence that water companies in the UK are also seeking to differentiate between classes of customers by developing more individually focused methods of analysing demand. A report by the Environment Agency, for example, showed that water companies were increasingly interested in the detailed dynamics of demand. The number of monitoring schemes focusing on domestic consumption increased from 5 in 1980 to 10 in 1988, and to almost 30 in 1994 (Turton, 1995, p14). Such interest suggests a new emphasis on the tailoring of water supply to match different profiles of customer demand. Some UK water companies are now developing new pricing incentive schemes to encourage the conservation of water in so-called 'green tariff' schemes. Strategically, the call for more imaginative tariffs, which recognize the need to balance water savings with social considerations has been backed by regulators. The Environment Agency has, for example, conducted extensive research into new tariff options for metered water supply (Pezzey and Mill, 1998). Tariffs might be used to differentiate water users and to distinguish between different types of water use, such as essential or non-essential, and peak or non-peak uses. The Office of Water Regulation (OFWAT) has stated that metering and tariffs are important tools for managing demand for water, especially where increases in consumption are driven by discretionary use such as garden watering. A number of water companies are now looking at designing tariff systems to be 'economically, environmentally and socially responsible' (OFWAT, 1997).

An increasingly popular view among local authorities and municipalities is that differentiated tariffs for waste services could create incentives for waste reduction. In many cases charges for waste collection and disposal are passed on through local taxes. Another approach is to replace standardized levies with billing systems based on the amount of waste that is produced by each household. The usual method of charging does not offer an incentive for people to separate or reduce their household waste. In response, the Dutch Ministry of Environment has developed more elaborate models of tariff differentiation (TD). Waste service charges have been revised to include a fixed small standard charge plus a variable part that depends upon the amount of waste to be taken away. In several field experiments the variable part was either based on weight, on volume and frequency of collection, or on the mandatory use of expensive waste bags. An evaluation of TD in 14 municipalities including all three methods was made by an independent research institute (Zelle and Van der Zwaan, 1997).

Results from surveys recording residents' opinions on the TD system showed that the majority of respondents would prefer to pay a fixed standard charge. People were reportedly afraid that the system would turn out to be more expensive than conventional charging approaches. Such expectations can change; later surveys showed that 50–55 per cent of participating citizens were satisfied with TD. The effectiveness of TD may be further impeded by evasive behaviour – so-called 'waste tourism' in which residents carried waste to neighbouring municipalities or to the workplace.

Evaluation

Product and tariff differentiation and metering in liberalized utility markets is generally designed to manage demand and/or to establish distinctive services intended to appeal to different sectors of the consumer market. There is no doubt that many more imaginative green tariffs have been introduced. The main difference compared to pre-liberalized markets is that utility providers have been able to differentiate between groups of customers (green and normal electricity customers, metered and non-metered water consumers, taxed or charged waste producers). In all cases, the choices available to individual 'customers' depends upon how they are viewed and positioned by different service providers.

CITIZEN-CONSUMERS IN DIFFERENTIATED UTILITY MARKETS

Examples of typical citizen-consumer roles in contemporary utility provision schemes are not difficult to find. Citizen-consumers may choose green electricity or become a member of a windmill association; they can separate waste fractions and bring them to different collection facilities; and they may have a rainwater butt in their backyard to water the garden. What is distinctive about *citizen*-consumers is that they are not adopting these practices for their own well-being. Instead, they have the deliberate and explicit ambition of making electricity and water supply or waste management a bit greener.

In The Netherlands there are about 20 windmill co-operatives representing some 6000 household consumers who are shareholders of one or more windmills installed by the co-operative itself. Wind power is transported to the electricity grid and sold to the energy distributor in the area. Profits derived from the exploitation of a windmill are re-invested in the installation of new turbines, as most members of windmill co-operatives state that they do not see this as a financial, but rather as an environmental, activity (www.ecn.nl, 1999).

The same arguments are advanced by green electricity consumers who take care to inform themselves about how and where green electricity is generated before making a choice between providers, prices and services. For such citizen-consumers, there are a number of small intermediate providers who buy from producers and offer mixes of solar, wind, hydro or biomass generated green electricity according to consumer preferences.

Citizen-consumers in The Netherlands now have a range of ways to deal with different fractions of waste. For example, bio-waste can be composted, paper and glass are recycled, batteries and chemical waste can be collected separately and so forth. Obviously a differentiated and well-organized waste management system needs to be in place to offer all these routes of domestic waste disposal.

Consumers and waste service providers in the UK also face a constantly expanding range of choices. Households are consequently obliged to make many more judgements than ever before. Should they take their bottles back to the shop for reuse; should they turn their organic waste into compost for the garden; should they transport their old clothes to textile bins at the supermarket or participate in the local newspaper collection service? Some UK commentators suggest that recycling is an increasingly important route through which people seek to maintain an identity as a green citizen-consumer. Hill (1996) describes the transition of recycling in the UK from a minority activity, 'a liberal trendy fetish or pursuit of the eco-crank' to a 'social movement, a common cause and part of everyday life'.

On the other hand, diverse and conflicting images of UK household waste management are emerging. For example, committed recyclers of the Bath 'Blue Box' scheme are to be found washing and segregating every item of the waste stream before carefully disposing of it in a range of different coloured bins (Hill, 1996). Elsewhere, less fastidious households may segregate recyclables but take less care over their 'purity', requiring further 'decontamination' of the waste stream. Others put all of their rubbish in one mixed bin on the grounds that responsibility for segregation rests firmly with the waste utility.

There is no one simple model of preferred consumer involvement across the UK waste sector. New household responsibilities (for instance, to separate waste) are almost always shaped by the specific objectives of waste utilities seeking to reinforce their particular service networks. For example, some collection authorities may already be locked into contracts with disposal companies that require the delivery of mixed household waste to centralized materials recovery facilities (MRFs), where different 'streams' are separated. In contrast, advocates of community-based schemes seek to encourage households to separate waste streams at source, perhaps as part of a process of environmental education or to save time and money.

Since privatization of waste services during the late 1980s, new commercial actors have entered the field. Again, responsibilities, service options and choices have been reconfigured. The contemporary coexistence of contrasting strategies reveals tensions between proponents of bottom-up approaches (conferring environmental responsibility on the household) and those that revolve around centralized, mechanized systems of waste management. The service decisions made in different areas have clear consequences for household arrangements, and for the long-term viability and development of different waste management regimes.

Evaluation

Differentiation in contemporary utility services in the UK and The Netherlands (in terms of resources, providers or technologies) may provide certain consumers with new opportunities to build social and environmental considerations into the ways in which they handle waste or consume electricity or water. But the extent to which consumers can manage their role as citizen-consumer depends upon the local configuration of service systems, waste collection and disposal sites, and political support for different scales of waste management. Being a citizen-consumer may well be combined with being a customer of utility companies or a co-provider of utility services.

CONSUMER-PROVIDERS IN DIFFERENTIATED UTILITY MARKETS

Consuming electricity or water and disposing of waste, while at the same time producing these services on one's own premises, is not something entirely new. Households have often collected rainwater for garden watering or composted their own waste. Here we consider how contemporary changes in utility systems have introduced and extended forms and techniques of co-provision.

Some households have the space to install a wind turbine and some have found their way through the labyrinth of municipal licences and regulations required to get these technologies up and running. Most energy companies now pay an equal price for delivered and consumed electricity on the net, regardless of the amount of kilowatt hours (kWhs) involved. Wind turbines are generally only an option for farmers and other rural inhabitants; yet other techniques are available for co-provision on an urban scale. Relatively easy applications at the household level are photovoltaic (PV) panels and micro-combined heat-and-power (CHP) systems. These technologies enable citizen-consumers to generate their own electricity without being disconnected from the main electricity grid. On the contrary, a grid connection remains essential as back-up and as a means of selling back any excess electricity produced.

Although the use of PV in the built environment is still quite rare, PV technologies are gradually diffusing into housing and building sectors. After a period in which solar panels were simply attached to existing homes, architects who specialize in sustainable building are now willing to incorporate photovoltaics within their designs. In The Netherlands, municipalities, developers and energy companies have been collaborating in several building projects to apply photovoltaics in residential areas with varying success (Van Mierlo, 1997). Whether willing or not, householders figure as the co-providers of electricity as long as the panels on their roofs produce enough electricity to send back to the grid.

Since 1999, a number of Dutch energy companies have introduced SunPower schemes, consisting of four photovoltaic panels and inverters and including the costs of installation on the roof. The set is connected to the domestic electricity system using a normal socket, making the electricity meter run backwards if more electricity is produced at a given time by the solar array than is being used in the house. Any kilowatt hours of electricity produced are thereby credited against the households' consumption ('net-metering'). The expected electricity production is 300–350 kWhs per year, which amounts to about 10 to 15 per cent of the average electricity consumption of one household. The real price of four panels was much higher than the 2300 Euro for which it was offered; but subsidies by the Ministry of Economic Affairs and the energy companies together lowered the price to almost 1225 Euro (Remu, 1999). In this, the SunPower system appeared to be fulfilling the goals that Greenpeace wanted to achieve with its Solaris project, launched in 1998 – namely, to create a breakthrough in the market and to get the price per panel lower than 450 Euro (Greenpeace, 1999). By launching an information and reference desk and by recording consumers' interest in solar panels, Greenpeace showed that there was a significant consumer market for PV energy. In March 1999, there had been requests for 15,000 panels. The SunPower system proved to be an effective instrument to keep the niche market for PV panels in the hands of utilities. As such, it illustrates how energy companies are broadening their business, not only selling electricity but also providing a broad range of energy-related services.

Home composting is another form of co-provision. In many municipalities in both the UK and The Netherlands, composting bins have been provided at a reduced price or distributed free to stimulate the practice of waste separation and composting (Going for Green/Tidy Britain Group, 1998). This can save municipalities the cost of collection and treatment of a large fraction of domestic waste (200 kg per household per year in one case in the Netherlands; IPH, 1998) and offers garden owners their compost as a free fertilizer.

A last example of co-provision is the practice of rainwater collection for domestic use. A Dutch water manager (interview WMO, 1999) explained that selling and maintaining rainwater systems to his customers fits well with the business strategy of specializing in water technology and water services. Stimulating the diffusion of rainwater systems is not necessarily an impediment to normal business, especially when the water company wishes to shift its core business from drinking water supply to some kind of general water service provision. The rainwater systems that have been installed in The Netherlands have a good record: rainwater appears to be very suitable for washing clothes, and because of its low calcium content it requires less detergent. Householders who use these systems state that they really like the idea of using rainwater for washing and flushing. In the sustainable building site 'De Bongerd' in Zwolle, a householder stated that 'at every downpour, there is the satisfying prospect of yet another rainwater laundry' (Holtsprake, 1998).

Rainwater systems have never been installed to save money. With current prices for tap water and rainwater systems, the investment will only be cost effective after 30 to 60 years of usage, depending upon subsidies for installation (Chappells et al, 2000). Yet, rainwater systems do allow households to decrease their dependence upon large technical systems and they give people the satisfaction of not 'wasting' water that is of drinking quality. If households install rainwater systems, roughly half of their water needs could potentially be provided by rainwater.

Evaluation

New forms of co-provision have emerged partly, but not entirely, due to the differentiation of utility markets and new regulations that finally recognize consumers as service providers, especially in the case of green electricity production. Co-provision of water, electricity or waste management may be intended by committed consumers, but may also be imposed upon them by providers who seek to shave peaks in demand. Hence, relations of co-provision can also be found among captive consumers, customers and citizen-consumers.

DIFFERENTIATION AND CONSUMER CHOICE

This chapter has explored some of the forms of differentiation that can occur within network-bound systems of provision. Differentiation of sources, providers and technical arrangements generate multiple possible consumer roles with respect to provision. Having explored some of the possibilities with reference to Dutch and British water, electricity and waste sectors, it is now possible to be more precise about what these developments really mean for consumer choice.

Many new consumer roles are largely the outcome of various forms of differentiation in utility sectors, rather than the result of explicit consumer choice. The differentiation of resources and providers sometimes enables consumers to take social and environmental issues into consideration. In fact, being a citizen-consumer has rarely been as 'easy' as it is today. The possibility of becoming a citizen-consumer is, however, dependent upon exactly how utility sectors are structured and, hence, what options they offer and foreclose. Likewise, 'choosing' to be a co-provider is only possible if regulations and markets make this possible. In some instances, there is no choice but to be a co-provider, while in other cases consumers may meet severe resistance when they try to become a co-provider on their own. In general, consumers are 'allowed' to choose their role as long as it fits the demand management strategy of providers and regulators. Meanwhile, mainstream utility practice is now such that consumers (being either in their captive, citizen or co-providing role) are increasingly treated as valued customers. In that sense, utility markets appear to be more and more like 'normal' markets. The problem is that 'normal' markets typically serve normal consumers, who may make irrational, or calculated, or committed, or even very unpredictable choices: something traditional utilities might find rather hard to cope with.

Having addressed the issue of differentiation and choice in general terms, we move on, in the next chapter, to consider questions of scale. By relating this discussion of 'differentiation' to the subsequent analysis of 'scale', we bring a new perspective to bear on the long-lasting debate about the relative social and environmental merits of small-scale versus large-scale provision.

NOTE

1   Case studies were conducted within the framework of the Domestic
    Consumption and Utility Services (Domus) research project (Chappells et al,
    2000). In this chapter we also refer to some interviews with utility
    managers, as well.

5

Shifting Scales and the Co-production of Green Grids

The cases of environmental innovation in utility sectors discussed so far indicate a diversification in the 'scales' of technological systems that are utilized in the generation, storage and use of energy, water or waste services. Along with these developments, modes of organization seem to be shifting from highly centralized top-down arrangements towards more decentralized management strategies, involving intermediate actors and end-consumers.

The call for decentralized technologies is nothing new. The environmental debate on the provision of infrastructure services, such as water works and energy supply, has long been dominated by the controversy between advocates of small-scale decentralized technology, on the one hand (Schumacher, 1973; Lovins, 1977), and defenders of Fordist modes of organization and large-scale networks, on the other. Schumacher's 'small is beautiful' thesis was based on the assumption that human needs and the environment are better served by small-scale technologies and systems of management rather than large-scale technological systems. Lovins suggested that energy systems can develop along hard and soft pathways. He regards the dominant hard path, characterized by a reliance on non-renewable resources, centralized management structures and large-scale grids as an inflexible and ideologically rigid mode of organizing and managing electricity supply. By contrast, he argues that soft paths, comprising localized energy networks and renewable energy sources, matched to specific end-use needs, are able to achieve greater efficiencies by minimizing distribution losses and the need for spare capacity (Chappells, 2003).

Economists are generally rather cautious regarding the decentralization of infrastructures as its supposed advantages should at least compensate for the loss of economies of scale (Estache, 1995).

This debate over small and large provision works with rather limited definitions of 'scale' focused around extreme possibilities of network configuration. The claims are also highly normative about the relative benefits of alternative options. While Schumacher assumed that smaller scales of provision would better meet the social and environmental needs of users, Lovins's hard paths are believed to be inherently inflexible and to foreclose softer options.

Two issues emerge from this. The first is: what is small and what is large? Anyone who has been in the proximity of a modern wind turbine would be impressed by its size. Yet, would the same wind turbine still be regarded as large in terms of electricity production and, especially, when compared to other electricity generators? There are no hard definitions for 'small' and 'large' as their meanings are relative. The matter is further complicated by the fact that apparently small technologies might only work in combination with huge technological networks. A car might be small compared to other modes of transport (planes, trains); but if we include the necessary infrastructure of roads and petrol stations within the definition of a car, it is anything but a small-scale technology.

The second striking issue is that the brief sketch of the dichotomy between small- and large-scale provision of infrastructure services shows that the debate refers not only to (the scale of) technology, but also to (the scale of) its social organization. There is, of course, nothing new in the idea that technological change can only be analysed if its social organization is included in such a study. However, it seems that the discussion of optimal scales of energy, water and other network-bound systems rarely goes beyond the technological parameters. The techno-logical scale of a system is too easily assumed to be managed by a social organization of a similar scale.

This chapter argues that contemporary environmental renewal in networks of water, waste and energy service provision sometimes challenges the assumed relation between scale of technology and scale of management and use. The labels 'monopolist provider' and 'captive consumer' no longer suffice to describe the more complicated social relations within network-bound provision of environmentally relevant services.

As 'scale' is too generic a term, the next section distinguishes four dimensions of scale that might help to analyse aspects of socio-technical differentiation within network-bound systems. To illustrate the relevance of distinguishing such socio-technical dimensions, two cases are presented: the first a sustainable housing project in which the residents experimented with 'down-scaled' water technologies; the second, a project of solar electricity generation on the roofs of one of the largest new-built residential areas in The Netherlands. The third section discusses the implications of different scales of organization for the roles and responsibilities of both providers and consumers of energy, water and waste services. In conclusion, it is argued that it is time to abandon the dichotomy between 'small' and 'large' in network-bound service provision, and replace it with concepts that more appropriately reflect the differentiated social and technical relations in these increasingly complex systems of provision and consumption.

FOUR DIMENSIONS OF SCALE IN UTILITY SERVICES

Changes in the form and scale of supply technology do not necessarily disturb the essential features of a network-bound system. Services might still be provided by mostly state-owned organizations. Equally, consumers might still be anonymous users, charged via fixed rates or taxes for the services provided. However, diversification in scales of the 'hardware' often goes hand in hand with diversification of the 'software': the practices of consumers, providers and their mutual relations. Different small- and large-scale providers have a wider range of roles to play in the provision of services than was formerly possible. In many cases, consumers may now decide to switch between providers and to choose between a differentiated palette of services. However, diversification in scales of technology does not automatically imply parallel diversification in terms of management or ownership. Indeed, most of the recent large-scale technological innovations, such as biomass power plants, are operated by utility companies, while small-scale innovations such as low-flow cistern devices and energy-efficient light bulbs are most often installed and used by individual consumers. Inverse relations between technological scales and the organization of management and ownership are also possible. Provision through large-scale networks might be 'splintered' into distributed generation and more autonomy on the local level, while the organization of the whole system might, at the same time, be even more up-scaled.

In trying to assess the implications of differentiating scales of water, electricity or waste service provision for consumer-provider interactions, we distinguish four dimensions of scale. First, technical scale or physical size is one of the factors determining the possibilities of co-provision. Second, there is the scale of management, influencing whether or not end-users will be involved in the provision of services. The reach of a system, thirdly, is a dimension that is largely overlooked when thinking in terms of small- versus large-scale provision and points to the impact many small (consumer) initiatives may have on big systems. Whether technologies can be applied on a stand-alone or a grid-connected basis is the fourth dimension that directly relates to how consumers and providers of infrastructures interact.

Scale of technology

This is the most common understanding of 'scale' – an understanding that simply refers to the size of the artefacts involved. Small-scale solutions for environmental problems that replace large-scale technologies include the composting toilet, the solar cooker, human-powered lamps and radios and so forth. 'Small-scale' usually refers to the size of the artefact or to its use on a local level, and in many cases to both. Small is considered even more 'beautiful' if it is also 'simple', which is often characterized by a technology that is easily constructed from local materials and can be maintained without the help of highly qualified technicians. In the environmental debate, nuclear power stations, oil refineries, wastewater treatment plants, landfills, intensive cattle breeding and many other industrial activities are generally considered large-scale technologies.

Scale of management

The degree to which the scale of technology corresponds to the scale of management can be observed in high-tech innovations in energy and water infrastructures. A small-scale energy generation unit such as micro-combined heat and power (CHP) or a system of on-site anaerobic treatment of wastewater can be managed and maintained not by individual consumers, but by the larger expertise organizations that have installed these units in the first place. By agreeing leases and contracts with service companies, users of those small-scale units assure themselves of the trouble-free functioning of these systems. Apart from the fact that generation or treatment units are of a physically smaller scale, the management of these systems is similar to that of large-scale utility systems.

An example of the opposite situation (large-scale technology with small-scale management organization) is the exploitation and management of a wind turbine or wind park by one or more owners and users. All over Europe there are windmill owners (individuals and associations) who sell their excess capacity to energy utility companies.

Not only can the number of actors or size of organization involved be an indicator of the scale of management, so too can the level of expertise needed to run a system. In some cases, lay knowledge may be sufficient (as in the case of maintaining a solar panel); in other cases expert knowledge is required to keep a system running (for example, micro-CHP).

The reach of a technology

Artefacts may be small, but they might be used in such volumes that their reach is large or extensive. A normal bicycle is a small-scale device in several aspects: it is a stand-alone artefact, used and maintained locally, and generally does not need much expertise or knowledge to run. However in the case of The Netherlands, it is used by millions of people as a day-to-day means of (urban) transport. In this respect, the reach of the bicycle is far from small scale. The massive use of bikes has also triggered the building of urban infrastructures such as bicycle lanes and stands, repair shops, road signs and long-distance cycling routes. In a different case, should composting toilets ever become a success, it would require the development of large-scale infrastructures of compost collection, handling and reuse.

Stand alone versus fully grid connected

A related issue that further complicates the conceptualization of technological scale is whether a small-scale artefact can function as a stand-alone device, or only performs if it is connected to a larger socio-technical infrastructure. The size of technological systems is highly determined by the interdependencies between the system and other systems. A bicycle may, for instance, still be a stand-alone technology in that one can still ride a bicycle in the absence of bicycle lanes. A wind-up radio may be a stand-alone device in terms of its energy use; but without the ether network of radio frequencies, it would be of no use at all.

To summarize: debates around scales of technology and, especially, the social expectations that come along with them would be more useful if reference were made to different dimensions of scale. In relation to the liberalization of utility markets, this is especially important as the conventional dichotomy between small (supposedly being beautiful or environmentally sound) and large (supposedly being economically efficient) does not suffice. This is particularly the case given that processes of liberalization have triggered socio-technical differentiation and the creation of niche markets of local or green utility-service provision with mixed scales of technology or management. The meshing of grids has become much more complicated: it is not a matter of being either small or large, we now see combinations of sub-grids within larger grids, with shared responsibilities between consumers, providers and many intermediate agencies. The implications of such differentiated systems for relations between the providers and consumers of energy, water and waste services is illustrated by two cases of environmental innovation in which one or more dimensions of scale have been altered.

Small-scale waterworks in a sustainable homes project

The first example is the water supply system in *Het Groene Dak* (the Green Roof), a Dutch ecological housing project of 66 homes initiated in 1989 and opened in 1993. The most innovative measures in this project were those taken to minimize the consumption of tap water in two shared apartment blocks (Chappells et al, 2000). Residents were successful in their lobby to the housing corporation and local water company to have a rainwater collection and distribution system installed in order to supply water to washing machines; composting toilets that do not use any water for flushing or require a connection to the sewer; and a grey-water tank, reed-bed filter and retention pond for all other wastewater treatment. It is clear that this is a case of down-scaling of water provision technology in several dimensions.

First, with stand-alone toilets and the on-site generation of water and treatment of wastewater, the technology of waterworks is scaled down from conventional large-scale water supply and sewerage to the household level. Only the supply of water for drinking is left to a network provider: the local water company.

Second, residents had responsibility for the daily management and maintenance of the installed technology. The composting toilets needed much maintenance, especially compared to normal flush toilets, and the composting process was to be monitored carefully. Residents learned that it was a rather uncontrollable process, but installed new ventilation, drainage and other devices to improve it. The remaining sludge needed to be dug out from the tank and reused in their garden or disposed of in other ways. The rainwater recovery system worked without any problems. Distinct from 'normal' drinking water supply, rainwater is collected, distributed and used in one location. Residents are therefore not only consumers, but also their own water providers.

A third dimension of scale is the societal reach of technologies. The project was only one of a few sustainable housing projects located in the midst of conventional housing areas at the time, and its impact on the world of centralized water works was only marginal. However, it was deliberately set up as an exemplar project: the initiators wanted to learn from their experiences and extend it to future initiatives. Their experiences were systematically listed on a website, including detailed tables of water quality indicators, and water and electricity consumption levels (www.groenedak.nl). The continuing story of maintenance problems in the case of the composting toilets was also well covered. The project became infamous when the residents decided to get rid of the composting toilets after seven years of failure. Much to the annoyance of the project initiators, they found that due to the possible risk of explosion or contamination by accumulated gases within the composting tanks, only professionals wearing protective clothing and gas masks could do the demolition. The picture of white-suited and gas-masked professionals breaking down a supposedly 'eco-friendly' toilet was published in national newspapers and achieved national TV coverage. Since the public failure of the system in *Het Groene Dak*, compost toilets seem to have vanished from the sustainable building agenda in The Netherlands.

The fourth and last dimension of scale refers to how and to what extent technologies are connected to larger-scale infrastructures or grids. The initiators of the *Groene Dak* project were eager to become as independent and self-sufficient as possible in terms of water use. At first sight, the rainwater system and composting toilets are, indeed, stand-alone devices since no grid connections are needed. However, drinking water is still supplied in the conventional way and may also be needed for back-up provision in times of drought or in case of technical failure. As the composting toilets did not produce reusable compost, the remaining sludge had to be disposed of through the municipal bio-waste collection and treatment chain. Avoiding the use of a sewer system essentially transferred the burden to the bio-waste collection system. In environmental terms, this might be a better option; but in terms of being self-sufficient and independent of large infrastructures, this is not necessarily the case. The residents of *Het Groene Dak* experienced that in urban housing projects it proves very difficult, if not impossible, to avoid connection to larger infrastructures.

Solar panels in a variety of grid connections

A second example of a diversified set of scales of socio-technical organization concerns the application of solar (photovoltaic) panels for electricity generation. Solar panels are small electricity generators that can be applied at several scales: from stand-alone appliances, as in the case of beacons, to grid-connected solar power stations in which thousands of panels may be linked together. In terms of ownership and management arrangements, the variety is almost endless. In Amersfoort, The Netherlands, the regional energy company is the owner of thousands of solar panels that are installed on the roofs of new-build houses (the '1 Megawatt Project', as described in Chappells et al, 2000). The generated electricity is either transferred to the central grid (and delivered to all clients in the region) or directly delivered to the householders living underneath the solar roofs. Other arrangements comprise a set of solar panels that can be purchased from the energy company and installed on individual roofs. The generated electricity is used in the household, while the excess can be 'sold' to the energy provider by configuring the meter to run forward or backward according to levels of sunshine and domestic consumption (net-metering).

As for the socio-political reach of solar panels, most developments (including the Amersfoort project) depend upon local, national or European subsidy programmes because the electricity generated remains more expensive than that generated by other sources. The share of solar energy in the contemporary green electricity market is therefore marginal compared to, for instance, biomass and waste-to-energy conversion. However, compared to other 'green' sources, solar power has an almost blank record when it comes to disputes about its environmental soundness. Contrary to biomass-based electricity production, there is no greenhouse gas emission in the conversion of sunlight into electricity, and unlike wind turbines there is hardly any problem of siting or landscape pollution. Moreover, having a solar panel on one's roof does much more for the green image of a household than participation in green electricity schemes. Such symbolic attractiveness of solar energy helps to enhance the reach of the technology, for its reach would be negligible if only economic considerations were taken into account.[1]

Solar panels are typically flexible when it comes to grid connection – the fourth dimension of scale. When used on a stand-alone basis, mostly with a battery for energy storage, solar panels are distributed as 'solar kits'. For example, donor projects provide a framework to establish electricity supply in the rural areas of developing countries. Real stand-alone appliances are, however, the exception and not the rule. Although there are no electricity lines to connect to, the user is almost always dependent upon proper battery maintenance and supply of spare parts by third parties.[2]

Most solar panel applications, especially in less sunny areas such as the UK and The Netherlands, do need a connection to the electricity grid for back-up. Excess electricity produced on long sunny days can then be delivered to the central grid, while all the other days can still be comfortable due to electricity supply from the grid. Such small generators dispersed over the network contribute to the distributed generation of electricity. The network no longer accommodates only a one-way supply of electricity from central power station to individual consumers, but a two-way road of supply and demand based on dispersed electricity generation and consumption.

The micro-power revolution as foreseen by Dunn (2000), among others, places great emphasis on solar panels and other environmentally sound innovations that need to be run on a smaller scale than the contemporary central power plants. Different from the Schumacher school that strives for self-sufficiency, micro-power presupposes a large-scale network to accommodate the two-way road of supply and demand. In such a new constellation, the categories 'small' and 'large' no longer suffice because the energy, water and waste networks combine small and large in several ways, making it impossible to draw a clear line between small- and large-scale applications.

ROLES AND RESPONSIBILITIES OF CONSUMERS AND PROVIDERS IN DISTRIBUTED UTILITY-SERVICE PROVISION

If the dichotomy between small- and large-scale does not suffice any more, what can be said about the roles of providers and consumers in new constellations of distributed energy, water or waste provision? Our two examples of small-scale water works and solar panels help to address this question.

As indicated, the *Groene Dak* project was set up as an exemplar project, and for this reason residents put much effort into monitoring and publishing data concerning the use of the various new technologies and materials. An illustration of this reflective approach is given by a resident who was the main initiator of the water-saving technologies in the project. After some years of usage and experimentation he came to the conclusion that in terms of environmental impacts related to water consumption, it is best to rely upon supply from a centralized water provider. Although the rainwater collection system worked very well, it was based on an electric pump system that distributed water from the basement to the attic. The compost toilets may have saved a lot of water; but they also consumed substantial amounts of electricity due to the drainage and ventilation systems that were installed in attempts to

71

improve the composting process. A comparison of the measured kilowatt hours (kWhs) used per saved cubic metre of water and the required energy usage to supply a cubic metre of conventional drinking water supply showed that the latter is much more energy efficient (twice as efficient in the case of the rainwater system and even 20 times more in the case of composting toilets; Post, 2000). The initiator concluded that on environmental grounds it is inefficient to rely upon the alternative water systems that were applied in *Het Groene Dak*.

Although this example provides only anecdotal evidence, it demonstrates how highly committed consumers of utility services have attempted to redefine their position towards conventional providers and systems of provision. As the case of solar panels and green electricity also illustrated, less 'active' or more 'ordinary' consumers might find themselves wondering if, how and to what extent electricity should be produced and delivered from centralized or decentralized sources, and who should be responsible for producing it (including the option of being a self-provider).

The 1 Megawatt Project in Amersfoort is designed not only to experiment with photovoltaic technology, but with various kinds of ownership and client–provider relations in energy provision as well. To allow investigation of the effects of various forms of ownership and management, the local energy company owns half of the installations. Agreements have been made with the developers concerned, which include accessibility of the installations and liability for any damage. A right of superficies (building right) has been established in respect of the plots. It has also been stipulated that the solar panels should remain un-shaded (which restricts the planting of large trees in front of one's home). The residents are remunerated by the energy company for the exploitation of their roofs. Twenty per cent of the energy generated on and from their roofs will be paid for at the normal domestic consumer tariff.

The other half of the solar power installations in Amersfoort are the residents' property. The solar power generated is fed into the main grid and, in return, residents receive the normal domestic user tariff for delivered solar electricity. This is a scheme with future potential: in an evaluation, the energy company stated that it does not intend to implement the former scheme elsewhere. Managers suggest that too much expertise was required for roof construction, which is not the core business of an energy company (interview REMU, 1999, cited in Chappells et al, 2000).

Processes of diversification of scale are likely to continue in the electricity sector (see also Dunn, 2000; Truffer et al, 2002), as electricity is a flexible, easily transportable form of energy provision. With co-generation systems such as photovoltaic panels on consumers' roofs, and more possibilities ahead, such as fuel cells and micro-CHP, the electricity grid is partly transferred into a storage system of redundant electricity that is produced at the household level.

SCALE AND MODES OF PROVISION

Different scales of technology and of socio-technical organization and moves towards distributed generation are associated with changing relations between the consumers and providers of utility services, but not in easily definable ways. As we have argued in Chapter 4, understanding these changes requires a closer reading of forms of differentiation – seen through the different technical, institutional, organizational and social arrangements that characterize national, local and household grids.

The assumption that the application of on-site technologies or distributed generation, in general, means that consumers gain power in their relationship with service providers should be critically assessed. Whether consumers gain power over how network-bound services are provided depends upon more than the size of technology or the scale of its application.

In analysing contemporary technology development in infrastructures of consumption, the use of a simple dichotomy of small-scale technology (supposedly being beautiful, environmentally sound and socially accept-able) versus large-scale technology (supposedly being economical, environmentally damaging and creating social inequalities) should therefore be abandoned. Liberalization of utility markets and privatiza-tion of utility companies did not bring an end to large integrated grids, even if it has involved their partial reconfiguration. Centralized control has not been dissolved; instead, responsibilities are now shared between many co-providing agencies. The trend towards decentralizing gener-ation with the application of smaller-scale generation technologies is counterweighted by the parallel trend of ever-increasing networks which connect all small generation technologies to each other (and which are centrally controlled). It is not the scale of technology that moulds the social relations between providers and consumers, but, rather, how the networks are being organized and managed. As a consequence, the relations between service providers and consumers should be defined in terms of different modes of 'distributed generation', 'network integra-tion' and 'co-provision'.

Having outlined the differentiation of consumer and provider roles (Chapter 4) and the shifting scales of technological systems (in this chapter), in Chapter 6 we address the new modes of sustainable provision that are partly made possible through these developments. In particular, we consider to what degree consumer 'autonomy' is enhanced.

NOTES

1 Solar panels are highly expensive as long as they are produced and applied on a marginal scale. Mass application would, however, lower the costs per watt peak – although prices of solar electricity have gone down from 6.26 Euros per watt peak in April 2002 to 5.97 Euros in October 2003 (www.solarbuzz.com/moduleprices.htm).
2 This represents the weakest aspect of these projects.

6

New Modes of 'Sustainable' Provision

Processes of privatization are generally associated with the increased 'autonomy' of consumers. As seen in Chapters 4 and 5, autonomy might relate to the ability to select between a range of differentiated products or service providers, or to become the producer of one's own energy or water. When thinking about sustainable housing initiatives, the concept of autonomy takes on a number of further dimensions.

For aspiring 'self-providers' or 'off-gridders', achieving autonomy requires the renegotiation of multiple social, institutional and technological dependencies upon mainstream systems of provision and the establishment of new technical grids and service regimes. Importantly, the development of new modes of provision implies much more than a reconfiguration of technical infrastructures – it also involves the re-evaluation of institutional and social conventions and environmental commitments.

New modes of provision can also demand a reversal of conventional utility-user roles as consumers become the providers of at least some of their utility services. This re-designation of consumers as 'consumer-providers' might also see them taking on board roles as the regulators, suppliers, financiers, service technicians and demand managers of their own mini-networks.

Our review of nine sustainable housing projects from the UK and The Netherlands is designed to identify different modes of provision, distinguished in terms of the character of social and technical attachments to conventional networks. Interviews with the initiators of our selected schemes are used to show how their chosen systems and methods of utility management relate different ideas about what autonomy and sustainable living involves and what it means for traditional dependencies between utilities, users and technical grids.

In particular, we consider how the social and technical dependencies being constructed in different situations involve various degrees of 'autonomy' from conventional systems of utility management. We also examine the relative success of different initiators in integrating environmental innovations and social practices to create new sustainable service regimes and contexts for more flexible and responsive forms of demand management. Our analysis of new network arrangements shows how attempts to dissociate from mainstream grids are tempered or mediated by the social and material characteristics and dynamics of the specific systems in question and by wider political and institutional arrangements.

SUSTAINABLE HOUSING INITIATIVES

Although large-scale infrastructures and centralized institutions are now generally considered the 'normal' mode of provision for energy, water and waste throughout much of Europe, this model of social and technical organization is not the only one possible. As discussed in Chapter 3, early utility systems often featured localized arrangements in which households had little choice but to self-provide. A number of consumers and providers are today reviewing their dependencies upon mainstream utility systems for reasons other than those of necessity. Even though infrastructures now reach the remotest of locations, sustainable housing providers cite a variety of social and environmental considerations that have influenced their decisions to construct mini-grids at the household and community level and to create new service systems.

In Europe, there is a long history of communities who have developed alternative ways of living, usually involving reorganizing some aspects of utility provision (Fairlie, 1996; Bunker et al, 1997). One of the most publicized examples in the UK is the Centre for Alternative Technology (CAT) in Wales, which was developed during the early 1970s as a 'living community to test emerging alternative technologies'. In The Netherlands, two equally long-standing projects are *De Kleine Aarde*, a centre for sustainable living, and *De Twaalf Ambachten*, where alternative technologies such as composting toilets are developed and demonstrated. In all of these projects the provision of energy, water and waste services involves some form of self-provision and management. The wires, generators, bins, grids, pipes and disposal sites that characterize these developments are often vastly different from those found in more conventional homes.

Interest in sustainable housing and in the development of new modes of water, energy and waste management has intensified since the 1990s (see, for example, Bhatti et al, 1994; URBED, 1995; Gwilliam et al, 1998). A variety of national and European policy and planning legislation and guidelines have been produced to support the development of such initiatives, including the Sustainable Communities Plan in the UK (2003) and a National Sustainable Building Centre in The Netherlands (since 1996). The European Commission has also focused on questions of how to promote more sustainable modes of housing provision and urban development (EC, 1999).

In line with these developments, many more 'mainstream' institutions – including property developers, house builders, utility companies, local authorities and housing associations – are now developing their own interpretations of what sustainable living might involve. Social housing providers have, for instance, developed sustainable homes that incorporate a number of passive design features and resource-saving technologies in an effort to save their tenants money and to improve the efficiency with which resources are used (see Hastoe Housing Association, 1997; National Housing Forum, 1997). More experimentally, some private property developers and house builders have combined environmentally innovative design and construction techniques with in-house computer systems in a number of 'smart home' or 'eco-tech' projects (Haddon et al, 1997; Clark, 2001).

As these examples indicate, what constitutes a 'sustainable' home or a 'green' mode of provision is open to a very broad range of interpretations. In respect of 'eco-neighbourhood' projects, Barton (1998) suggests that rhetoric of sustainability is generally one that invokes 'human-scale, mixed-use and socially diverse neighbourhoods, providing residents with increased convenience and [a] sense of local identity, while at the same time reducing their ecological footprint' (Barton, 1998, p162). A further objective for many of those involved in initiating such projects is to achieve 'a very high degree of local autonomy' (Barton, 1998, p162).

Such representations of 'sustainable living' do not necessarily hold for all developments and the modes of provision being developed are likely to vary widely, reflecting the social and institutional objectives and priorities of initiators and households (who may or may not be one and the same). As Guy and Osborn (1997, p192) argue, 'green buildings can be conceptualized as social representations of alternative ecological values or the material embodiment of different discourses that make up sustainable living debates'.

Extending this argument to the scale of sustainable housing projects, our case studies show that those involved in constructing new modes of provision favour different models of sustainable living, each of which embody different ideas and objectives concerning degrees of autonomy from conventional developments, aspirations to comfort or convenience, and desires for social or environmental distinction. Specifically, we show how the 'green' aspirations and objectives of different providers and consumers become infused or embodied in the specification and operation of utility management systems within different sustainable housing schemes.

The values and commitments of those constructing sustainable housing schemes will not solely determine how utility management systems are defined and used. Existing institutional and infrastructural arrangements also influence the extent to which initiators and users of new sub-systems are able to create new modes of utility management (Hughes, 1983; Summerton, 1994). Developing such arguments, Jensen (2001) shows how existing infrastructures influence the concept, configuration and location of 'green buildings'. In many cases, these make it difficult to connect (or disconnect) from networks and construct new regimes of flow management (Jensen, 2001). These arguments are equally relevant when considering efforts to plan, construct and connect sustainable housing projects and to expand it with new modes of energy, water and waste provision.

By examining relations between sustainable homes and mainstream infrastructure networks we hope to reveal how long-standing socio-technical dependencies and ties are being stretched, severed and realigned around new models of sustainable living, and what this means for the conceptualization and practice of utility consumption and provision. As well as affording consumers a range of opportunities to dissociate from conventional providers and grids, new network arrangements redefine consumers' roles as supply-and-demand managers. In the final part of the chapter, we reflect upon how the new socio-technical constellations we have identified are associated with strategies of demand management that require different degrees of commitment from consumers and providers.

CONCEPTUALIZING NEW SOCIO-TECHNICAL ARRANGEMENTS

Initiators of sustainable housing projects range from those who are seeking to alter their own household sustainability (as individuals or part of cooperatives), to groups who are developing sustainable homes but not living in them (these include architects, housing associations and

	Technically disconnected	Technically connected
Socially disconnected	Type 1: aim to be self-reliant and develop low-tech/alternative technology removed from conventional systems. Example: *eco-communities* – communes that provide their own fuel, food, water and are closed to outsiders.	Type 2: aim is self-sufficiency, but homes are still connected to conventional technical systems. Example: *self-build communities* – communities who provide their own fuel and waste systems but still retain attachments to grids.
Socially connected	Type 3: aim is not self-sufficiency and conventional social relations are maintained, but developments include technically off-grid features. Example: *social housing schemes* – aim is to fit with local social identity, but to have self-managed systems.	Type 4: conventional social and technical connections are maintained and reinforced with high-tech solutions. Example: *future 'eco-tech' homes* – smart homes with high-tech control systems linking utility functions.

Figure 6.1 *Types of social and technical connectedness*

municipalities). In those developments where the initiator is 'remote', in the sense that they do not live in the homes, social and technical arrangements are likely to differ considerably from those found in 'self-initiated' projects. Equally, households living in homes designed by private developers are likely to be afforded different degrees of independence compared to those living in social housing schemes. 'Autonomy' is also likely to take on different meanings in relation to different schemes. In some situations, self-providers might seek to retain a connection to mainstream networks, whereas in other situations they may attempt to disconnect entirely.

Figure 6.1 illustrates the different degrees of social or technical connectedness or disconnectedness we might encounter in different types of sustainable housing development.[1] By 'social' connectivity we mean whether participants in sustainable housing see themselves as 'normal' consumers or providers, or whether they regard themselves as somehow special cases whose aim is to 'disconnect' from established social and institutional networks. In terms of 'technical' connectivity we are referring to a physical relationship to utility grids and whether systems are actually disconnected from mainstream networks. In the typology, both social and technical connectivity are treated as relative categories. Our intention is to capture the variation in these levels, not to assign sustainable homes to strict types.

Those schemes included in the first segment of our typology (see Figure 6.1) would include developments in which there is a strong sense of social and cultural detachment from mainstream provision networks, and in which initiators seek more self-sufficient homes and lifestyles. In turn, these initiators would aim to sever technical connections with conventional networks, setting up their own mini-grids on-site. Initiators of those schemes positioned in our second segment see themselves as distinctive from conventional providers with regard to their social and environmental aspirations, but would aim to retain or even strengthen technical connections in order to ensure the eco-efficiency of the project (for example, by selling electricity back to the grid). Initiators of schemes positioned in our third segment would view sustainable utility provision as something that could be achieved by maintaining conventional relationships and social ties with mainstream providers, but might seek to achieve some degree of technical autonomy via the implementation of experimental decentralized systems (such as on-site grey-water recycling systems or wind generation). Finally, sustainable housing initiators might maintain or even reinforce connections to national and regional grids, using the latest technical equipment to optimize their relations with conventional providers (type 4).

This simple typology serves to show that initiators and users of sustainable homes are faced with a range of possibilities in selecting the new technical and social frameworks within which they want to reconfigure ways of life and methods of utility provision. Unlike many 'normal' homes where social conventions and technologies are already well established, the decision to build greener homes in some way implies a range of new choices.

In examining case studies of sustainable housing our aim is to identify and examine the different types of socio-technical interdependencies or interconnectivities that are emerging between environmental technologies, providers and households across sectors and countries. Drawing upon the insights and experiences of initiators, we revisit arguments about the extent to which new networks of provision can be conceived of as socially and technically 'autonomous' from conventional arrangements. Furthermore, we consider how the new utility management conventions, routines and practices associated with these systems are redefining meanings of consumption, provision and demand management.

CONSTRUCTING NEW SOCIO-TECHNICAL INTERDEPENDENCIES

Interviews with the initiators of nine sustainable housing schemes were used to examine the ways in which modes of utility provision are being socially and technically restructured. Discussions with these informants were also designed to reveal the conventions and principles of service provision and demand management that each new network arrangement embodies. The cases were selected from a wider inventory of environmentally innovative housing schemes (see Raman et al, 1998) on the basis that they each feature different degrees of social and technical autonomy from conventional networks.

In the UK, we interviewed the initiators of five projects as detailed below:

- *Allerton Park*: a self-build development of three houses in a suburb of the city of Leeds in Yorkshire. The initiators aim to achieve social and technical autonomy, especially in relation to water and sewage systems.
- *Hockerton Housing Project*: a development of five self-build earth-sheltered houses initiated by the families themselves. The homes can be seen to be socially off-grid, with intentions of gaining autonomy from water and energy systems; in reality, they are still connected to some conventional technical systems.
- *Harlow Park Ecolite Homes*: the Ecolite Development was initiated by the CDS Housing Association in Liverpool to 'test and extend options for water and energy efficiency' and to meet the needs of tenants who had campaigned for improved housing for ten years (see Evans, 1997). The 23 new homes are in Toxteth, an inner-city community where space is at a premium.
- *Bryce Road Development*: this 15-home scheme was initiated by the Black Country Housing Association in Dudley, West Midlands, and represents phase one of a scheme to build lower environmental impact houses at a low cost for social housing tenants.
- *Integer Housing*: Integer is a group of architects, building professionals and housing organizations whose aim is to build the 'green and intelligent' houses of the future. The Integer show house is a smart home with high-tech control systems linking utility functions. Fitting more closely to our socially and technically connected model of autonomy (see Figure 6.1), the development maintains and reinforces conventional utility relations using high-tech solutions.

In The Netherlands, four projects were selected for study:

- *Het Groene Dak*: an ecological housing project in Utrecht self-initiated by residents of 66 homes. The aim is to encourage energy and water savings through combining conservation measures, including water-saving taps and showerheads, and insulation. A small number of households have been conducting a small-scale experiment with composting toilets and grey-water recycling in an attempt to achieve technical autonomy from the main sewer system.
- *Polderdrift Housing Association*: a housing development in Arnhem initiated in 1992 when a municipality competition was held to come up with ideas for a sustainable building project. There are 40 houses; but only five of the original initiators have stayed. The premise is for low-rent houses for families and the elderly with more space, but a lower 'ecological footprint'. Most eye-catching is the communal rainwater and grey-water recycling scheme with reed-bed filters in the project's communal garden.
- *De Bongerd*: a development of 36 properties developed by a housing co-operative in the town of Zwolle in The Netherlands. The homes feature rainwater collection systems, solar-heat collectors and on-site recycling. Households retain connections to conventional grids.
- *Amersfoort*: this housing development in the district of Nieuwland includes a zero-energy balance solar-demonstration home and a large-scale development of over 500 homes where different solar and other environmental technologies are being tested (called the '1 Megawatt Project'; see Chappells et al, 2000). A social monitoring survey has been undertaken to assess the scope for integrating solar innovations at different scales (see Sylvester, 1998).

Examining all nine cases allows us to compare the philosophies and practicalities of institutional and technical restructuring in different social and political contexts. In each case we visited initiators on-site. Our enquiries were designed to elicit information on five aspects of social and technical interdependency, as detailed below.

Technological interdependencies

A first objective was to understand the technical ingredients of 'sustainable' homes and to examine the history of choices behind each. We focused our enquiries on how technological choices interlocked, whether environmental innovations were piecemeal or part of a package, and how new devices interfaced with existing infrastructural arrangements.

Interdependencies between providers, users and new technologies

Our second concern was to understand the relation between providers, consumers and newly established infrastructural arrangements. Here, we concentrated on the extent to which the introduction of new technologies prompted the renegotiation of provider and user roles in service provision and introduced new opportunities for demand management.

Social interdependencies

A third issue we considered was the extent to which initiators and self-providers see themselves as 'normal' or different from mainstream consumers, and how specific social and environmental values and concepts are woven into the 'sustainable' systems and modes of provision that they construct.

Institutional and political interdependencies

The degree to which the decisions of sustainable housing providers are structured by their attachment to particular institutional and political systems is another important consideration. Aside from providers and users, options for utility management are influenced by a range of institutional 'intermediaries', including building regulators and local authority planners. Networks of plumbers, electricians and other local experts also influence the ongoing integrity of sustainable housing projects. The realignment of responsibilities between sustainable housing providers and these external agencies is assessed.

Dynamics of dependency

A final set of enquiries focused on the dynamics of changing dependencies and on questions of how and why grid connections and social dependencies are being reviewed over time.

With these issues in mind, we now examine the types of interdependency that were being developed and renegotiated in our nine sustainable housing schemes.

Technological interdependencies examined

Most of the homes we investigated included a basic pack of technical ingredients – extra insulation, high-efficiency boilers, advanced glazing systems, reduced-capacity cisterns, water-saving taps and recycling bins.

These technologies appear to be synonymous with a range of 'sustainable' modes of provision. Some of the homes we visited also contained more novel and experimental technologies. For example, in the Bryce Road development, sun pipes were used to provide natural light for dwellings and in Harlow Park, experimental grey-water systems were installed in four of the houses. In the Integer demonstration, home innovative and state-of the art features were incorporated, including an in-house smart-metering and energy-monitoring system. Self-initiated projects included many more experimental technologies, with reed beds at Hockerton and Allerton Park and composting toilets at *Het Groene Dak*. In such projects, issues of orientation, storage area and slope were often important, as was the need to link technologies to the spatial design of homes.

Technologies, whether tested or experimental, simple or complex, old or new, were carefully evaluated by initiators in order to take into account their 'fit' with other household devices, systems and structures. One way to unpack these relationships of technical interdependency is to consider what happens when a technology breaks down and to think about the 'back-up' systems that can be implemented. In some of the self-initiated projects, there was resistance to dependence on mains back-up unless it was absolutely necessary, leaving many new technologies to stand alone. For example, in the Allerton Park homes, the rainwater system for drinking water was initially set up to provide for all of the water needs of the families. This technological independence was challenged one winter when the pipes froze, leaving households with two options: to sit it out and wait for the thaw, or to revert back to mains supply. Two of the three households chose the latter option and in doing so reaffirmed the interdependency of mains water systems with those of self-supply. In the Hockerton project, two back-up systems for heating are in operation. During cold winter nights when solar energy systems fail to provide enough heat there is a mains supply of electricity to boost temperatures; the alternative 'technology' is to put on extra clothing.

In almost all of the projects technological trade-offs were made. A number of self-providers described the dilemmas they faced in deciding whether to buy the most energy-efficient appliances or to take into account embodied energy used in manufacturing and keep hold of old appliances until they wore out. In other cases, the integration of some technologies negated the use of others. For instance, in *Het Groene Dak*, the initiators thought they could link high-efficiency furnaces and solar heaters, but were unable to do this because the devices were incompatible.

Decisions about the water reuse technologies reveal differences in self-providers' ideas about appropriate scales of provision. Often initiators were strongly in favour of one system or the other. For example, at *Polderdrift* in The Netherlands, eight households shared a rainwater system, while at Allerton Park in the UK each household had their own supply tank. The selection of individual or shared water tanks was, perhaps, the most contentious issue for self-providers since it implied the revaluation of concepts of cleanliness and hygiene, as well as overcoming physical difficulties related to on-site storage.

In the 'remotely' initiated schemes, heating systems were often a subject of contention. For example, despite reassurances by the initiators of the Harlow Park development that central heating systems would not be required as a back-up to passive ventilation and solar technologies, many tenants insisted on their inclusion. The provision of 'booster' technologies in almost all of the projects we visited illustrates the extent to which formal and informal ideas about 'acceptable' standards of heating co-exist, and how particular infrastructural arrangements reflect social expectations and conventions of comfort as much as ideas about what is technically or economically efficient. In Zwolle, the initiator explained that the technological options selected were the result of negotiations about how to achieve 'eco-possibilities without losing comfort'.

Interdependencies between providers, consumers and new technologies examined

In the Harlow Park development, the simple action of replacing a light bulb reveals new dependencies between the housing association and the tenant. The brochure handed out to tenants explains that:

> Your home has special fittings for low-energy light bulbs. These are not the same as you would buy in the shops for a traditional fitting, but will be considerably cheaper and last three to five years. Please speak to your housing officer about buying replacement fittings, and for advice on lampshades (CDS Housing, 1999).

In this case, the simple task of changing a light bulb must be negotiated with the housing provider, and consumers are 'locked' into a new relationship of dependency.

Other remotely initiated schemes offered further insight into the extent to which social and technical dependencies and responsibilities are being renegotiated. In the Integer Homes, there are dual logics of dependency in operation, revolving around concepts of pre-fabrication and 'ease of adaptation'. On the one hand, a number of pre-programmed water-efficiency features come ready made in a bathroom module, which would be difficult to replace or modify. At the same time, there are access hatches all over the house so that tenants and repair people can easily adapt wiring and light settings. This 'green and intelligent housing' model may offer the least scope for consumers to replace technologies, but provides a large variety of programmable options.

In the examples described, it appears that the level of consumer autonomy is dependent upon the extent to which providers are willing to delegate responsibilities to users and upon how successful they are in importing their own notions of sustainable living into the design of technologies that lock consumers into certain modes of operation.

There is a differing degree to which technical arrangements in specific sectors are physically 'fixed' and how this influences options for the reconfiguration of service regimes. The renegotiation of responsibilities for managing waste, which is relatively mobile in comparison with water and energy, appears to involve more open processes of negotiation between tenants and providers. Households can either choose to deal with waste collection themselves, as in visiting local 'bring' sites, or make a contract with a local waste collection company to provide this service. In Harlow Park the solution involved four on-site stores for the disposal of different types of waste with collection by the local council. In Zwolle, underground containers were supplied, and tenants were provided with special electronic cards that allowed access to stores. It enabled tenants to monitor and regulate patterns of disposal. Whatever the method chosen, there appears to be more flexibility in how households choose to deal with their waste and in how far providers are willing to support these options compared to water or electricity service provision.

Social interdependencies examined

The scheme we identified as being most socially disconnected was Allerton Park in the UK. Here, the decision to achieve more 'autonomous' lifestyles related to a complex set of cultural, social and environmental beliefs. One of the initiators explained that the group had a number of shared commitments and values, including 'mistrust of the system, search for radical alternatives, individualism, and the environmental notion of keeping everything in our own valley'.

A common social referencing system used by self-providers was to talk about the 'normal' or 'straight' world as set apart from their world. A resident of one UK project explained that they considered grey water 'too extreme' and reed beds 'too much' for more conventional households. The ideas of initiators and consumers did not always mesh when it came to issues of social and environmental distinction. Although initiators were generally keen to promote the green identity of their schemes, some encountered resistance from tenants who did not want to be seen as 'different' from their neighbours. In the Ecolite development in the UK, this was illustrated when households requested that timber framing – a symbol of ecological living – should be confined to the back of the homes only.

Social aspirations and priorities varied widely. A number of self-providers expressed the sentiment that they wanted to 'do something different'. For example, one of the initiators of *Het Groene Dak* explained that others should follow their model, but should develop their own interpretation of sustainable living. The adoption of what were seen as 'socially off' notions by 'straight' actors, such as utilities, was seen by some self-initiators as weakening the spirit of independence in green projects. The sense of 'recreating' a strong sense of community was supported by the Zwolle initiators who wanted it to be 'as it was in the early days: meet your neighbours in the corner shop'. The strongest socially connected story came from the Integer project, where the initiator's aim was to provide low-cost alternative housing as part of a wider plan to develop new 'greener and more intelligent' approaches to 'volume' or 'mass' house building in the UK.

The on-site servicing arrangements of sustainable households reveal a great deal about the ways in which relations between new service arrangements are being reviewed and reconstituted. In self-build homes, including Hockerton, contracts were often made to reflect new obligations between the consumer-providers. The inclusion of individual household meters meant that if an irresponsible resident left a tap running and drained the on-site reservoir he or she would be penalized. In this case, households have set up a maintenance and services company to formalize ties between residents and demarcate responsibilities. In other developments, such as Zwolle, the choice of individual rainwater systems is considered fairer. This arrangement means that smaller families do not suffer from overuse by larger ones. In *Polder-drift*, potential residents were screened by the housing association to assess whether they would be willing to participate in the collective management of on-site systems and resources. At Zwolle, there was no obligation to buy 'green' appliances; but there was some degree of 'informal' pressure by fellow tenants. The brochure describing what it is like to live at *De Bongerd* leaves residents in no doubt about what counts as acceptable behaviour: 'Living in *De Bongerd* is . . . to smuggle your tanning bed, microwave and other "wrong" devices into your house during the night.'

Institutional and political interdependencies examined

We have already noted that self-providers set up new legal entities and maintenance agreements that mirror contractual arrangements between 'normal' users and conventional utility providers. Our interviews further revealed that the independence and autonomy which initiators often hoped to achieve from conventional utilities and institutions were hard to realize.

Self-providers argued that current supply standards and regulations restricted what they could do. In the UK, residents of Hockerton explained that they have to pay a registration fee if they are to sell excess energy back to the grid. Given the small amount of electricity likely to be produced, this requirement has forced them to reconsider the cost effectiveness of becoming an exporter of power. For self-providers at Allerton Park, existing water-quality regulations and standards – designed to protect consumers – made it difficult to establish an off-grid drinking water supply. In this case, water regulators insisted on stringent independent monitoring of drinking water quality that households found time consuming and difficult to maintain. Another example of how conventional utilities influence the environmental integrity of schemes comes from *Het Groene Dak*, where residents agreed to separate their plastic waste for collection by the local utility company, only to find out that plastics were mixed together later in the waste disposal chain.

Current regulatory frameworks were not the only problem. Many initiators of green building projects explained that contractors and trades people did not always share their enthusiasm for new design features and technologies. Plumbing and building contractors were often reluctant to work with 'new-fangled' innovations. In Harlow Park, the architect described how the building contractors 'resisted almost everything that was different from conventional homes', including the design of bin stores, canopies and a communal garden. Initiators at Hockerton explained that electricians wanted to revert to 'normal' wiring with PVC. In these examples, another set of interdependencies emerge between 'conventional experts' (builders, plumbers and electricians) and sustainable housing initiators. As the Zwolle Housing

Association points out: 'Living at *De Bongerd* is ... to build a close relationship with your troublesome rainwater pump and with the plumbers.'

Relations between conventional trades people and sustainable housing initiators varied considerably among different projects. In the case of the Integer home, social relations are maintained and reinforced with high-tech solutions. Many of the technologies included in the demonstration home are 'state of the art' and initiators' reliance upon outside 'experts' for maintenance is considered crucial. Initiators explained that there was a real concern about who would be around when things go wrong, and about a likely lack of local 'fixers'. The sophistication of systems and the amount of expertise associated with them clearly shapes the relation between residents and external institutions.

Some proposed innovations challenged the existing regulatory regime. In sustainable building projects such as Integer, the initiators – including architects, property developers and building research groups – were able to exert high-level pressure on the government to force regulatory change. The initiator interviewed described how they 'decided to go to the top, the housing minister and the prime minister' to get change and to 'bypass the resistors'. By contrast, the initiator of *Het Groene Dak* explained that they 'were not allowed to talk to people in power', and had to work through mainstream housing corporations, who they felt were 'diluting' their ideas. For the initiator we spoke with, every stage of the project was a political struggle – from 'breaking into the city plan' to orientate the houses for solar energy, to getting agreement to transport water between them. A similar argument was made by initiators of *Polderdrift*, who explained that they had started off with ambitious plans, such as using rainwater for showers, but ran into resistance from the housing association that represented them.

With respect to funding for new projects, initiators explained that conventional mortgage lenders are often reluctant to finance sustainable building schemes, especially those that are considered too socially and technically disconnected and, hence, too risky an investment. The Allerton Park scheme was only possible with the help of a specialist ecological building society, while other schemes, such as Hockerton, were largely self-funded. The lack of conventional sources of funding to support such schemes was considered to be one of the main barriers to achieving different degrees of autonomy in the UK. Initiators further noted that conventional utility companies sometimes offer small 'pots of money', but generally only for the experimental elements of sustainable homes, such as water recycling units or solar collectors. Many initiators argued that utilities are only interested in sustainable housing projects as real world 'test beds' for new technologies. This was most striking in the Amersfoort development where the entire housing estate was a 'test bed' for solar energy. Future schemes were unlikely to be supported to the same extent.

Systems of billing and payment were also considered relevant in shaping possibilities for the future reorganization of modes of provision. In Polderdrift, despite residents managing to reduce the volume of their waste going to central sewage systems by 85 per cent, they complained that they still paid the same amount for this service as everyone else. For these aspiring self-providers, uniform systems of charging clearly presented a significant challenge when trying to make sustainable systems pay.

Dynamics of dependency examined

In the cases we have reviewed, social and technical relations were continually being renegotiated and degrees of autonomy were reassessed. As sustainable housing projects evolve, dependencies are further realigned and adapted. For instance, the early breakdown of water systems in Allerton Park resulted in a shift from a 'technically disconnected' to a 'technically connected' position, as some residents reconnected to the mains. In *Het Groene Dak*, the technical connectivities also shift significantly, with the reconnection to mains systems, most notably in the case of sewage. In this case, when the residents found that the waste from their composting toilets was useless for reuse on their gardens, they took the unconventional route of disposing of it in their wheelie bins for collection by the municipality. Social and institutional dependencies in this scheme appeared to have shifted the most, the rationale changing from one of self-provision to a preference for centralized provision by conventional institutions.

The dynamics of adaptation also reflect different individual and collective thresholds – relating to the extent to which consumers are willing to live with the inconveniences associated with new forms of service provision. In many cases, there is a period of readjustment in which residents are prepared to persevere with new systems despite their idiosyncrasies; but after a point, they cross a certain threshold of acceptance and reconnect to old systems. Residents' personal and collective thresholds vary depending upon the service or system under threat, but in some cases can seriously challenge the longevity of 'green' modes of provision.

The extent to which consumer-providers are willing to renegotiate financial thresholds is also important. The cost of installing grey-water and rainwater systems ranged from UK£500 to £2000. In the Allerton Park development, where the system had been constructed from cheaper components, the price of the rainwater system was at the lower end of this scale. The estimated saving for each household in this case was UK£150 per annum. The Harlow Park homes cost 2.4 per cent more than conventional homes of this type; but it was estimated that UK£50 a year savings in energy bills would make the investment worthwhile. These examples give some idea of the range of payback possibilities.

Initiators and residents of different schemes had their own ideas about what constituted a 'sustainable' mode of provision; but perceptions and possibilities changed over time. In general, expectations of energy and water savings and waste reductions were lower than expected in the first year, though initiators remained confident that ratios would improve. For example, in Zwolle, first-year water savings of 25 to 30 per cent were recorded with an expectation of 40 to 50 per cent, while in Hockerton households had reduced energy usage by 80 per cent, but hoped for further reductions once new equipment was brought on-line. Many of those we spoke to were continually revaluating their understanding of 'sustainability' and questioning how much of a saving was enough to constitute a credible 'green' system of provision.

Finally, patterns of disconnection often related to the institutional and political dynamics of the wider 'macro' utility world. For instance, in the case of Allerton Park, the decision to introduce rainwater systems was partly attributed to residents' objections to the privatization process. The initiator we spoke with explained that the privatization of water services in the region and the perceived mismanagement of water by their regional utility company had prompted them to seriously consider alternative modes of supply. Equally, the inclusion of grid-connected solar panels in the Amersfoort development was only made financially possible because of European Union subsidies and the local energy company's interest in developing and promoting new forms of renewable generation. In these cases, and in others, the decision to develop new modes of provision was bound up with local, regional and national politics.

The cases we have reviewed reveal wide variations in the socio-technical dependencies being worked out by providers and consumers of new sustainable modes of provision. As Figure 6.2 indicates, each scheme exhibits differing degrees of autonomy from the conventional world of utility provision. Strikingly, none of the initiators we spoke with claimed to have achieved independence from mainstream grids: each was still influenced to some extent by institutional conventions associated with centralized utility service regimes.

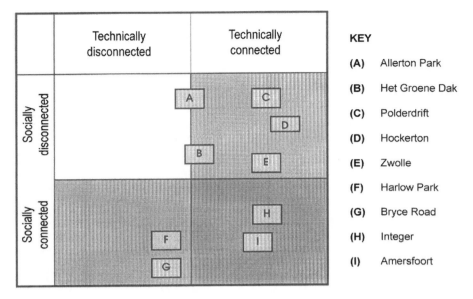

Figure 6.2 *Different modes of sustainable provision and shifting socio-technical connectivities*

In each of the sustainable housing developments we have looked at, initiators have defined distinctive frameworks for sustainable living and utility management that embody specific social and environmental objectives. The values and commitments of initiators may provide a template for sustainable provision, but they do not define the configuration and operation of systems. Modes of provision actually adopted also reflect the dynamic institutional, regulatory and political contexts in which they develop and the material specificities of the utility systems in question.

In the self-provider situations we have described the roles of consumer and provider have collapsed into one. Even where initiators are 'remote', consumers and providers are jointly implicated in redefining utility systems in sustainable homes through processes of negotiation, purchase, design, use and maintenance. At each stage, choices made by sustainable housing providers and users are structured by institutional rules and resources and by shifting personal and collective conventions and commitments. Initiators' decisions about the configuration of technologies 'lock' consumers into the reproduction of certain types of sustainable practice. Equally, in their roles as utility service providers, consumers challenge existing institutional conventions by making new types of 'green' connections.

Relationships between self-providers and regulators can be particularly contentious and may not be evenly balanced. For example, in the UK existing water-quality regulations made it difficult to establish an off-grid drinking water supply and regulations for the export of power proved to be problematic for small-scale renewable generators. As these examples illustrate, new modes of provision can be limited by regulatory frameworks designed for public provision and infused with certain notions of what constitutes a safe and efficient method of supply.

Although self-providers often seek autonomy from mainstream networks, this is rarely possible to achieve. At each stage in their attempts to get off-grid, initiators described how they came up against a variety of institutional, technical, material and political constraints. It is evident, on the basis of the cases discussed here and elsewhere in this book, that the potential for innovation and the scope for consumer involvement in constructing alternative systems of sustainable service provision are great. However, the extent to which new arrangements can be realized differs depending upon the details and dynamics of socio-technical interdependencies.

As represented here, different forms of self-provision are characterized by different degrees of engagement or disengagement from mainstream systems. Privatization has not led to the dissolution of centralized control, or the rise of the autonomous consumer-provider. Our cases of sustainable housing suggest that what we are seeing is a partial devolution with responsibility for provision now shared between many agencies, the objectives of whom sometimes conflict. We have observed the construction of many new types of sub-networks, most of which remain attached to the main grid in one way or another. Such findings are in keeping with the accounts of infrastructural change offered by writers such as Graham and Marvin (2001), who conclude that old and new network formations co-exist and that new sub-networks containing distinctive consumer and provider logics can be found operating within and alongside the conventional socio-technical frameworks embodied in mainstream systems.

To conclude, we briefly reflect upon what this interweaving of sub-networks and mass systems means for consumers' roles in managing demand.

NEW MODES OF PROVISION AND THE RESTRUCTURING OF DEMAND

It is often thought that decentralized micro-grids offer more flexible opportunities for juggling supply and demand. In practice, and as the examples considered here demonstrate, forms of flexibility and responsiveness vary widely. Localized systems of self-provision are designed to ensure that certain household needs are met without excessive on-site storage capacity or back-up mains supply. In some of the schemes we looked at, the highly localized nature of energy, water and waste infrastructures means that balances between system capacity and demand are tight and unpredictable. Rather than building system capacity capable of dealing with all but the most extreme loads, households routinely adopted a range of demand management strategies, putting on extra clothes during cooler weather and taking fewer showers if required to flatten peak load. In practice, keeping within self-set limits involves sustained care, commitment and effort. Consequently, a number of the aspiring self-providers we interviewed have renegotiated their personal and collective relation to the main grid, usually opting for reconnection in order to meet peak-time demand and to manage in emergency situations. In other situations, initiators have quite different ideas about what sustainability or efficiency involves and might maintain or maximize connections to mainstream grids in order to achieve their particular demand-management objectives. In conclusion, we can say that each set of new household arrangements brings with it unique options for managing demand.

Our review of new modes of provision further reminds us of the extent to which material differences between energy, water or waste really do count when it comes to the structuring of choices and the management of demand. In the situations described above, water networks were generally more difficult to reorganize because opportunities for self-provision were constrained by regulations built upon notions of universal public-service provision. Although waste arrangements were generally more malleable, dealing with 'messy and smelly' components such as compost and sewage proved difficult without the help of mainstream institutions and infrastructures. Electricity generation can now be achieved at various scales and through diverse connections to the central grid. The energy utilities, however, remain the central players in electricity provision and trade. These cases also reveal the extent to which sustainable consumption depends upon the extent to which households and institutions are willing to revise ideas about comfort or cleanliness in order to meet new environmental commitments.

Building on arguments about service differentiation and scales of provision, this chapter adds another dimension to analyses of sustainable utility consumption. In considering sustainable homes, we have shown how micro and macro systems of socio-technical organization come together to create locally differentiated contexts for demand management that are continually reformulated over time. In the last of our empirical chapters, we look at how new concepts and strategies of demand management are working out within mainstream systems of institutional and technical organization.

NOTE

1   These different categories are identified from an inventory of sustainable housing schemes in the UK and The Netherlands (see Raman et al, 1998; Chappells et al, 2000).

7

Restructuring Demand and Efficiency

Cases of self-provision tell us something about how utilities and users are jointly implicated in processes of environmental restructuring. In this chapter, we explore cases of innovation in demand-side management (DSM): a concept that has come to inform utility management practices since the 1970s, and which, according to some energy policy experts, represents an opportunity for utilities to draw consumers back into view and engage them as the co-managers of demand, rather than the passive beneficiaries of supply (Gellings, 1996).

One feature of demand management is that it encourages utilities to account for the character of consumption in different locations, and to recognize the benefits that targeted load management schemes could have in 'stressed' areas of load growth or under-capacity (Siohansi, 1996). In this sense, examining cases of demand-side innovation promises to reveal the role of households and utilities in constructing, manipulating and managing demand in different political and geographical contexts.

Rather more ambitiously, this chapter sets out to reconnect debates about the restructuring of household systems of energy, water or waste management and about the restructuring of wider infrastructural and institutional systems. Following the suggestion of Patterson (2003), we analyse household infrastructures as part and parcel of the regional or national infrastructures and urban and rural systems in which they are embedded.

To begin, we say a little more about how demand-side management has developed as a concept and what it has come to mean for different utilities in different countries.

THE DEVELOPMENT OF DEMAND-SIDE MANAGEMENT

Until recently, the theory and practice of electricity, water and waste management in most European countries was almost exclusively focused on the sizing and provision of supply (Patterson, 1990; Winpenny, 1994; Guy and Marvin, 1995). Massive investment programmes dating from the beginning of the 20th century had put in place power stations, reservoirs and disposal sites designed to meet the growing needs of households, to guarantee public health and safety, and to promote economic growth. Stability and security of supply were the dominant concerns, as reflected in the practice of sizing networks in anticipation of future demand. These social and technical arrangements positioned providers as the managers and controllers of the entire system, simultaneously situating consumers as the passive beneficiaries of good quality water, increasingly reliable electricity supplies and safe methods of waste disposal.

Since the 1970s, new approaches to conceptualizing, organizing and operating electricity, water and waste networks have been developed by utilities and policy-makers; these take into account providers' abilities to manage as well as to meet demand (Patterson, 1990; Gellings, 1996; Siohansi, 1996). According to Gellings (1996), the concept of DSM and the programmes that it has inspired offer an opportunity to draw the consumer back into view and represent a significantly different way of thinking for utility managers, who previously had little interest in consumers or in the details of their demand. As originally envisioned by electric utilities in the US, DSM built customer needs more directly into the utility resource-planning process. The idea was that demand could be differentiated and, hence, manipulated in a variety of ways. Methods of DSM initially involved the adoption of a fairly specific set of techniques designed to flatten peak electricity load profiles. DSM has since become an umbrella term, describing various measures for increased efficiency, load or flow management and conservation (Gellings, 1996). What such approaches share is the aim of improving network efficiency without building extra production or disposal capacity, and without reducing the level of service to customers.

By the late 1980s, demand-side management had come to be regarded as a central aspect of network management in a number of countries and for a variety of reasons (Guy and Marvin, 1996). In the electricity sector, support for demand-oriented approaches has generally been triggered by problems of network capacity and growing concerns over the long-term sustainability and economic prudence of an energy strategy based on oil and nuclear power (Lovins, 1977). With respect to water, opposition to large-scale reservoir schemes and concerns over the costs of building and maintaining supply infrastructures have prompted interest in strategies such as metering (Leversedge, 1974; Rees, 1974; DOE, 1992). For waste, concerns over the siting and safety of landfill sites and over potentially harmful emissions from incinerators have called into question centralized and undifferentiated approaches to collection, treatment and disposal, and have highlighted possibilities for differentiating and recycling components (Gandy, 1994).

On the whole, the concept of DSM signals a redefinition of what service provision involves. As utility managers have come to appreciate that resources are only important for the services they provide, they have realized that there may be less resource-intensive means of providing the same services. Viewed from this perspective, measures to improve efficiency and increase the effective capacities of power stations, reservoirs, disposal sites and distribution networks sometimes make more sense than efforts to extend the supply infrastructure (Siohansi and Davis, 1989). Some utilities have also begun to take more of an interest in the character of demand in different locations, recognizing the benefits that 'targeted' schemes, designed to reduce demand in the most 'stressed' areas of the network, can have in negating the need for new supply capacity across the network as a whole (Siohansi, 1996).

In the context of this book, DSM represents a way of thinking about network management that recognizes interdependencies between consumers and providers, and the possibility of generating new coalitions of interest for the concurrent management of both supply and demand (Guy and Marvin, 1996). At the same time, it is important to recognize that conceptualizations of 'demand' and of 'efficiency' are highly variable, and that the precise meaning of 'demand management' reflects the specific historical and institutional settings in which strategies are defined and adapted. It is therefore important to understand the social and political context within which demand-management approaches have been developed.

DEMAND-SIDE MANAGEMENT APPROACHES IN THE NETHERLANDS AND THE UK

Some commentators have noted the comparative slowness with which European utilities initially embraced the concept of demand-side management, attributing this to a lack of appropriate economic, technical and regulatory incentives. In the UK water sector, for example, the scope for savings was seen as relatively limited compared to the US because domestic levels of demand were already much lower (Environment Agency, 1998). In addition, universal domestic water metering, seen as a key tool for implementing and evaluating DSM schemes in the US, was less widespread in both the UK and The Netherlands. In the UK electricity sector, price controls, which rewarded companies for selling more electricity, initially acted as a disincentive to pursue demand-side options (OFFER, 1992). Nonetheless, by the mid 1990s, demand management was being viewed as an integral part of British and Dutch energy, water and waste management by regulators and utilities alike.

Energy-demand management

In the UK electricity sector, demand-side initiatives have focused on the promotion and implementation of the Energy Efficient Standards of Performance (EESOP) programme (EST, 1994; OFFER, 1998). When initially introduced during the early 1990s, the EESOP programme gave each regional electricity company a target for 'lifetime gigawatt hour' savings to be achieved through the implementation of energy efficiency and demand-side measures primarily for domestic customers (OFFER, 1992). Projects initiated by UK electricity providers have included subsidizing and fitting insulation, providing more efficient heating systems for low-income customers and offering a discount on the price of more energy-efficient appliances or devices. A further objective of the EESOP programme, as originally envisaged, was to improve energy efficiency and conservation in areas of the distribution network where high capital costs would be incurred to meet small increases in energy demand (OFFER, 1998). In reality, such 'targeted' DSM projects have been relatively limited, one exception being the Holyhead DSM scheme (see Guy and Marvin, 1996). In The Netherlands, energy-demand management has been motivated primarily by environmental concerns (Boyle, 1996). Energy companies have subsidized the purchase of energy efficiency devices, insulation measures, high-efficiency heaters and solar collectors (Slingerland, 1999). In contrast to the UK, McEvoy et al (1999) note how The Netherlands has managed to use the cheapness of current energy prices as a positive opportunity for introducing environmental levies.

Water-demand management

Environmental regulators at the National Rivers Authority (NRA) initially played a central role in defining water-demand management approaches in the UK. They estimated that up to 20 per cent of the total water put into public supply could be saved through leakage control and the utilization of efficiency devices (NRA, 1994). The introduction of the UK Environment Act in 1995 further supported the shift to demand-side management and placed a duty on all water companies to promote the efficient use of water as an alternative to major supply works (DETR, 1998a; Environment Agency, 1998). This requirement was reinforced by the development of standards of water efficiency performance overseen by the Office of Water Regulation (OFWAT) (OFWAT, 2001). In The Netherlands, water DSM measures have also been initiated by environmental regulation. Policies to prevent the depletion of ground-water resources and 'desiccation' of natural reserves have forced water companies to close sites of water abstraction and to look for alternatives. Efficiency measures, including dual flushes on toilets and water-saving showers, have, in some cases, successfully postponed investments in new water extraction and treatment plants and the scope for DSM activities is increasing (Wolsink et al, 1998). These moves mark a significant shift in the orientation of British and Dutch water policy, regulation and management. The focus is no longer solely on building new reservoirs or extending abstraction licences; instead, water companies have been compelled to consider the benefits of reducing leakage by reinforcing pipe work and developing a range of efficiency schemes directed at end-consumers. In several of the most 'water-stressed' areas, utilities have initiated DSM schemes on their networks. For example, the UK utility company Yorkshire Water has promoted water efficiency in remote villages where mains supply has been intermittent in summer months and where political pressure has been most intense (Osborn and Marvin, 2001).

Waste-'demand' management

In relation to waste, demand-side management refers to the curbing of production in the home by generating less packaging or diverting some components to new, more efficient disposal sites, such as the compost heap.[1] A complicating element in talking about DSM in relation to waste is the fact that it is not a 'commodity' that is sold or provided in the same way as energy or water services. In the UK, for example, the cost for waste collection services is still embedded in council tax, so financial incentives for reducing 'consumption' are relatively weak. The rise of differentiated charging in The Netherlands is closer to the traditional model of DSM, utilizing rebates and other economic incentives to persuade households to reuse or recycle some components.

The reorientation of British and Dutch utility management in the ways described has far-reaching conceptual, as well as practical and political, implications. Instead of positioning consumers as the passive beneficiaries of universal energy and water resources or producers of undifferentiated bundles of waste, the implication is that users have a key role to play in actively shaping network efficiencies for different services and in reducing demand. At the same time, it is not clear what more demand-oriented approaches to utility management really mean for consumer roles in service provision. The translation of the broader concept of DSM into specific programmes of action, at least in The Netherlands and the UK, suggests that the promise of demand management as a strategy for radically reconstructing consumer roles in utility provision has not yet been fully realized. In both these countries the generic concept of DSM has become increasingly synonymous with a quite specific approach, one that restricts consumers roles to that of more efficient end-users. The majority of the approaches we have described, including the EESOP programme in the UK and the *Milieu Actie Plan* 1991–2000 (Environmental Action Plan) in The Netherlands, are designed to meet taken-for-granted standards of service provision. By implication, demand is positioned as a non-negotiable need that has to be met: the challenge is to achieve this as efficiently as possible.

One consequence of this formulation of 'demand' is that utilities and regulators take little account of how service expectations might reflect institutional norms and rules, associated with the development of perhaps now outdated modes of utility management. Another is that they fail to address how 'needs' might be reconfigured over the longer term as expectations change. Here we aim to show that 'demand' can be understood as an altogether more malleable and negotiable concept.

In Chapter 3 we identified a variety of modes of organization, each underpinned by a different conceptualization of demand as something to be nurtured and manufactured, to be curbed and controlled, to be manipulated and managed, or to be met at all costs. In examining cases of DSM innovation in the UK and The Netherlands, our intention is to show how these different models of demand and interpretations of network efficiencies inform the network management strategies of current providers and in what ways this allows consumers to act as the co-managers of demand.

NEW CEILINGS AND THRESHOLDS OF DEMAND

Although the emergence of DSM initiatives is linked to the creation of new contexts of consumption, there has been surprisingly little analysis of the multiple roles of consumers as participants in DSM strategies. Privatization has also triggered the reconfiguration of production interests. Utilities are no longer the only legitimate managers of energy, water and waste. Organizations such as housing associations and local authorities, for example, are negotiating and delivering new energy, water and waste services and systems for their tenants. Again, the multidimensional roles of these groups in structuring demand-management options has so far received little attention from utility researchers and policy-makers.

In order to unpack some of the new consumer–provider relations being constructed, we conducted interviews with the developers and initiators of a variety of DSM schemes in The Netherlands and the UK. Our empirical investigations focused on a number of innovative pilot schemes in what we considered 'hard-pressed' areas of networks – those where resources were physically or institutionally restricted in some way.[2] In each of the cases we review, managers have introduced new storage and efficiency devices in an effort to alleviate pressure on existing supply networks.

In our analyses of DSM innovation, we look at how technologies establish and sustain new physical or institutional 'ceilings' and service expectations that reaffirm certain models of network management. In this sense, we view storage and efficiency devices not only as containers or constrainers of physical water, waste or electricity flows, but also as carriers of institutional and social conventions or rules that structure and shape utility–consumer relationships and capacities for demand management. Looking at the role storage and efficiency devices play in the mediation of resources through utility supply chains reveals much about the material characteristics of domestic networks of provision and the structuring of demand.

Setting new physical and institutional ceilings

The capacity of local landfill sites, the regional water storage situation, the relative distance to local power stations and local weather patterns are clearly influential in defining approaches to demand management. The specific character of environmental strains or resource problems is likely to frame the strategies employed in each sector. It is equally obvious that provider-defined 'ceilings', by which we mean institutional limits on total reserves or available capacity, influence how utilities and users think about demand and structure what these groups can do, in practice. The environmental commitments of utility organizations, the structure of tariffs and payment systems, and regulatory standards for the building of new infrastructure are all relevant in this context.

The first point to emerge from our interviews with 'hard-pressed' managers was that many were not as restricted by 'physical' ceilings as we had assumed. In relation to waste management at Sutton Borough Council in the UK, we heard that there was no physical problem of landfill stress as planning permission had just been granted for a new landfill site: ceilings were, instead, shaped by high 'self-imposed' targets for environmental performance set by the council itself. The recycling manager we spoke with explained that the council's aim was to achieve an 80 per cent recycling rate by 2005 and to significantly reduce the proportion of waste going to landfill.

Water managers working at Gemeente Waterleiding (GWL) in Amsterdam further explained that 'there are no real ceilings; you can extract what you want', referring to the ease with which they could abstract surface water from the River Rhine. This was in contrast to those water companies operating elsewhere in The Netherlands who relied more upon groundwater resources. At Waterleiding Maatschappij Overijssel (WMO), the Overijssel water company in Zwolle, a ceiling was set on groundwater abstraction by regulators; therefore, despite the existence of plenty of water in the province, which could potentially be made available for use, abstraction was strictly controlled. Limits for these managers related both to the capacity of purification plants and to the rules set by the province of Overijssel.

Other providers took account of what their consumers could afford. Managers at one UK housing association explained that although they faced environmental pressure to conserve water and that there were difficulties with local abstraction, the main reason for attempting to limit water use was to minimize the cost to households. Here there was some resonance with self-provision communities, where the resource ceiling is self-imposed in a way that fits the household's water ethics rather than the absolute availability of water. For instance, at Hockerton and Allerton Park in the UK, households could reattach to mains water or ship in tankers to refill their reed beds. In practice, the decision to limit water use was shaped by household beliefs and values and by the goal of using water from 'within their own valleys' without relying upon outside help.

In all of these cases, the companies involved were restricted by a combination of political, economic and institutional pressures. In this sense, resource pressure is not a 'natural' but a socially constituted problem. By implication, the scope for managing demand depends upon how regulators, utility companies and households set limits. Significantly, all of the utility managers we spoke with mentioned the 'back-up' option of supply investment, but explained that to legitimize such investment they are required to 'show willing' or 'pay lip service to' demand-side options. For example, an Amsterdam water manager explained that:

> We are now using 95 per cent of our capacity, which is the maximum. We cannot infiltrate more water into the dunes, so we need another purification plant. This is planned already; but we need the permission of the city council, as well as the money. Expanding capacity will only be accepted by the public and policy-makers if we install water meters.

New storage devices and the reconfiguration of ceilings

Infrastructures are made up of a variety of storage devices – including huge water service reservoirs, local electricity sub-stations and kitchen bins. These receptacles and containers do not only have a practical function; as writers such as Akrich (1992) have discussed, they can also be conceptualized as mediators of social relations. In relation to infrastructures we might further envisage a chain of mediating technologies that each embody certain macro and mini 'ceilings' representing the priorities and investment decisions of multiple institutions.

For those configuring such devices, relevant issues might include the amount of time consumers will go without the certain services or the containment capacity needed at particular network points. Viewed in this way, configurations of bins, storage heaters, sub-stations and reservoirs take on new dimensions. The sizing of storage devices and time schedules inscribed in them are critical in influencing how providers and users define resource problems and how they perceive supply-and-demand management responsibilities. This can be demonstrated by considering some of the configurations of devices being developed and introduced by our 'hard-pressed' managers.

At Sutton Borough Council in the UK, the choice and configuration of storage technologies is central to how the waste resource problem is perceived and managed by domestic consumers. Here, households have been provided with a set of recycling bins, comprising wheelie bins for private households and larger communal bins for apartment blocks or small estates. The collection of recyclable wastes (including glass and newspapers) is negotiated with tenants who are responsible for maintaining their adopted waste deposit site (often located in private gardens or car parks). Households can deposit newspapers and glass at their own convenience. There is also a financial incentive as groups of residents are paid by the tonne for the amount of newspaper and glass they deposit. The council is faced with a problem, however, in that the market for (and, hence, the demand and income to be made from) old newspaper is notoriously uncertain. They could potentially ask households to adapt their deposits to match the changing demand for newspapers; but this would involve constant renegotiation of personal and collective 'thresholds' relating to issues of convenience and financial payback. As it is, the council absorbs market uncertainties itself, and adopts an approach where it maximizes 'collection of recyclables and find a way to deal with it'. This brings into play a series of sub-stores (transfer stations and materials recovery facilities) around which the council, on the householder's behalf, effectively 'absorbs' the waste problem.

Efficiency measures and the renegotiation of service expectations

If demand is viewed as a non-negotiable need that has to be met, utilities are unlikely to take much interest in challenging consumers' service expectations. Instead, vast reservoirs, landfill sites and large power stations will be built to ensure that consumers are provided with a guaranteed and secure supply with little pressure to re-evaluate dependencies upon utility systems or to modify demand. The introduction of more market-based approaches to DSM implies that consumers may be invited to reconsider their dependencies upon large technical systems. Some consumers, for instance, have been asked to accept interruptible supplies matched to particular financial incentives, especially at times of shortage. The introduction of devices for water, energy and waste efficiency further implies a realignment of responsibilities along the supply chain and a re-evaluation of service expectation.

Although efficiency devices rarely make a dramatic dent in the daily lives of consumers (we can still make a cup of tea in the morning with a water-saving tap and read our books at night time with an energy-efficient light bulb), their introduction does require some re-evaluation of consumer and provider roles and service expectations. These new arrangements also involve the fine-tuned reconfiguration of household infrastructures where stability has, until now, been the 'norm'. With the introduction of more and more efficiency devices, there is a real possibility that expectations of reliability or other standards of service provision may be further reconfigured to reflect new provider–user priorities.

This possibility is one that is acknowledged by the utility managers we interviewed. Many were attempting to keep networks as tightly controlled as possible; but they were also beginning to recognize the new challenges they faced in doing so. One UK electricity manager explained that while building a power station is seen as 'robust' from the utilities' point of view, demand-side measures, such as the distribution of energy efficient light bulbs to households, are less so because customers might not use them, or use them in places where there was no (need for) lighting before, or might not use them at the 'moment' that the utility expects or wants:

> The problem is that, whilst its an obvious connection to make that if everyone reduces electricity use by CFLs [compact fluorescent lamps], it defers the need for a new power station; there are things that you can't account for that make it so uncertain . . . one customer had an energy-efficient bulb in its box for a year because the old one had not worn out yet.

The introduction of devices to reduce water used to flush toilets is another particularly revealing example of how utility managers cannot always rely upon consumers as the co-managers of demand. The successful use of cistern devices such as 'hippos' relies upon the maintenance of 'normal' flushing routines. A number of the UK water managers we spoke to complained that such specifications were not always adhered to; evidence from their household monitoring programmes suggested that many users often flush twice, negating the environmental benefits of installing the efficiency device.

In highlighting such scenarios, utility managers acknowledge the importance of the concurrent scheduling of provider and consumer expectations and practices if demand-management objectives are to be achieved. The mismatch between provider and consumer expectations (and schedules) also has more far-reaching political implications. In a number of cases, the inability to predict consumer activity meant that utility managers were uncomfortable with the shift away from more robust and guaranteed networks of supply and were unconvinced of the value of DSM schemes that involve consumers (however tentatively) in the co-management of provision.

In other situations, demand managers explained that the introduction of efficiency and storage devices had been used to successfully offset localized problems of water supply. Managers at United Utilities in the UK explained that they had been refused a licence for borehole abstraction by the Environment Agency. Instead, the company had spent UK£200,000 on leakage and efficiency measures – including the promotion of water butts to be used for collecting rainwater for garden watering – all designed to offset the need for resource development. Managers estimated that this targeted DSM scheme had saved only one mega litre of water a day, but explained that this was enough to bridge any short-term deficit in water supply. Again, though, there was a sub-text to this story: the longer-term strategy for the company was still one of source enhancement in order to meet expected future demand.

The cases of storage and efficiency that we have described show how utilities and users are jointly involved in setting new micro ceilings and redefining personal and collective service expectations, some of which have wider ramifications for the macro organization of networks and the balance of supply-and-demand management techniques chosen. Providers configure and install technologies that, to varying degrees, mediate material flows and establish certain ceilings on resource use. These groups also construct certain service expectations and assumptions about efficiency and demand. Consumers play an equally active role in redefining socio-technical ceilings and service expectations, sometimes at odds with those imposed by providers. These cases show that options for demand management depend upon how different ideas about efficiency and reliability are structured through entire chains of technologies and practices.

THE STRUCTURING OF DEMAND

New technologies of storage and efficiency have the double promise of permitting greater consumer responsibility and flexibility, while also offering suppliers more opportunities to manage and manipulate demand. DSM may draw consumers back into view; but utility providers still have a considerable influence over the forms of consumer involvement that are possible.

In one sense, utility managers are the mediators of demand, buffering consumers from the 'natural' and economic uncertainties that characterize energy, water and waste management. We have described, for instance, attempts by providers to 'absorb' demand fluctuations and to standardize household behaviour in relation to recycling practices. This strategy contrasts with self-provider situations, where the 'fail safe' of utility back-up is removed and households face shifting resource problems that they must adapt to every day. Here, household expectations and practices are continually re-evaluated to ensure that networks and flows are maintained within relatively tight limits. By contrast, efforts to disconnect users from the changing intensities of resource problems in their local areas reflect a particular understanding of utility provision – one in which protecting consumers and keeping networks as robust and reliable as possible takes precedence over more intermittent approaches. For most 'mainstream' managers, the long-term logic remains one of supply expansion and reinforcement even if environmental regulation or localized resource problems have caused them to implement DSM strategies in the short term.

Utility companies are locked into a process of ceiling-setting across the supply chain, involving negotiations with regulators and consumers. New types of service providers increasingly shape these decisions. The restructuring of demand-management options will depend upon how far utilities are willing to accept less conventionally robust service regimes, embodying new concepts of efficiency or reliability. There is some evidence that utilities are still locked into rather more conventional logics of supply management, despite fulfilling their demand-side commitments to environmental regulators.

To conclude, we reiterate the point that demand needs to be understood as something that is highly negotiable and systematically configured, not as something that arises solely as a consequence of individual action, belief or choice. Focusing on the dynamics of ceiling-setting and threshold negotiation has revealed the extent to which consumers and providers are the co-managers of complex and highly interdependent socio-material systems that embody equally complex concepts of demand and efficiency.

NOTES

1 Another element of waste-demand management might be source reduction and environmental consumerism, which focuses on influencing the purchasing and packaging decisions of consumers (see Ebreo et al, 1999). Here we are concerned more with management of waste in the home and decisions regarding its storage or efficient management for disposal, recycling or reprocessing.

2 Interviews were conducted with 'demand' managers at the following Dutch and British utility companies: GWL (Amsterdam, The Netherlands); WMO (Zwolle, The Netherlands); Southern Water (UK); Scottish Hydro Electric (UK); Sutton Borough Council (UK); United Utilities (UK).

8

Systems of Provision and Innovation

At the start of this book we proposed that the development of 'greener' modes and systems of service provision depend upon new forms of interaction between utilities and users. In making this point, our intention was to deliberately reposition debates about the environmental restructuring of utility systems away from an approach rooted in the idea that socio-technical change can only be achieved through the transformation of individual consumer behaviour. Instead, we have argued for a conceptualization of infrastructural change as a systemic and collective process of reform involving both consumers and providers in the greening of provision and the co-management of demand.

Our thematic analyses of specific forms of environmental renewal show the relevance of viewing utility provision as an interdependent process linking utilities and users in processes of 'co-provision'. The illustrative cases we have described demonstrate how the choices, needs, capacities and service expectations of consumers and providers are influenced by the institutional and infrastructural systems in which they are embedded.

In this final chapter we summarize some of the unique relations, processes and dynamics of 'co-provision' identified from our analyses of environmentally inspired infrastructural change. We then reflect on the implications of our analysis for the conceptualization and practice of sustainable utility provision.

'GREEN' CONNECTIVITIES

Having examined cases of environmental innovation in Dutch and British systems of energy, water and waste management, we now revisit debates about what the reorganization of utility networks means for environmental action. Specifically, we address questions about whether the range of green 'choices' open to consumers is increasing and whether there are more opportunities for consumers to act as the 'autonomous' providers of utility services. In exploring themes of 'differentiation', 'modes' and 'scales' of provision and 'demand' management, we have been able to identify new configurations of consumer–provider relations and, hence, new possibilities for environmental renewal.

Restructuring opportunities: Power and potential

The fact that processes of restructuring have created new choices for consumers is not really in doubt – for example, it is only recently that domestic electricity consumers have been able to select their service provider or to buy green electricity. But does this signal an increase in consumer power? Not necessarily. The introduction of large-scale dual water systems in The Netherlands was apparently motivated by 'the wish of consumers'; but households were not participants in decision-making processes. The decision to withdraw such systems was driven by policy-makers' concerns about the potential risk to public health. Likewise, consumer-producers can now choose between a range of off-the-shelf micro-generation technologies (for example, photovoltaic cells, wind turbines, recycling units or home composters); but options for the installation and operation of these units are structured by mainstream institutions. It is clear that not all consumers are em-powered to the same extent. It is also apparent that the possibility of acting 'autonomously' varies considerably in relation to the system in question and in relation to providers' (as well as consumers') convention and perception of risk.

Scales of provision and the relation between consumers and producers

As we saw in Chapter 5, privatization and liberalization have created opportunities for the development of novel and niche forms of provision organized at a variety of scales. In analysing these developments, we argued that distinctions between small-scale technology (supposedly being beautiful, environmentally sound and socially acceptable) and large-scale technology (supposedly economical, but environmentally damaging and creating social inequalities) was misleadingly simple. Liberalization of utility markets and privatization of utility companies have not brought an end to large integrated grids, even if they have involved partial reconfiguration. Centralized control has not been dissolved; instead, responsibilities are now shared between many co-providing agencies.

It is not the scale of technology that moulds the social relations between providers and consumers, but rather how the networks are organized and managed. As a consequence, relations between service providers and consumers should no longer be defined in terms of a rhetoric of 'large-scale production' and 'small-scale consumption', but are more appropriately characterized with reference to different systems of provision, such as those involving 'distributed generation', 'network integration' and 'co-provision'.

Modes of provision and autonomy

The sustainable housing case studies considered in Chapter 6 showed that there are many interpretations of what 'autonomy' means in relation to utility provision. Compromises and trade-offs were routinely made between consumers and providers. These reflected contrasting understandings about what constitutes an optimal or efficient network. Degrees of social or technical 'autonomy' achieved by households depended upon how far different providers were willing to delegate responsibilities to consumers and upon how far conventional notions of what is optimal and efficient were already embedded in the design of buildings and technologies. Other actors – including local utilities, regulators, planners, plumbers and electricians – also played a role in defining service expectations and in configuring options available to 'marginal' providers. Different modes of sustainable housing provision illustrated a variety of new ways of combining niche and mass systems of provision. In many of the cases we reviewed, these appeared as complementary rather than alternative modes of provision. In thinking about options for more decentralized networks and infrastructures it is therefore important to consider shades of interconnectivity between new and old institutions, rather than a wholesale shift from one mode to another.

Mainstream and marginal contexts of demand management

The forms of demand management being developed today are influenced by formal and informal obligations, technical standards and expectations of service, and by the ceilings and capacities afforded by different technological arrangements. In some situations, as in Sutton in the UK, municipality waste managers took on an active role in absorbing resource fluctuations and in mediating demand. Paradoxically, examining the mainstream utility's efforts to develop demand-side measures showed that the dominant logic remains one of supply expansion and reinforcement. Only in this way did managers think that they could keep networks as efficient and 'robust' as possible.

Meanwhile, consideration of demand management at the margins of provision suggests that infrastructures can be reconfigured in ways that challenge this dominant 'mind set'. Self-providers cope with periods of intermittent supply by adjusting their clothing or rescheduling their activities, thereby challenging the convention that electricity or water supply has to be continuously and instantly available around the clock. The extent to which households adapt depends, in part, upon the duration of disruption to 'normal' service and the back-up systems available. Intensified demand pressures at certain moments can also shift the dependencies that different mainstream or off-grid arrangements have on each other. These experiences raise a number of more general questions about how expectations and conventions become normalized and about the circumstances under which providers and consumers might re-evaluate conventions of 'normal' practice or routine.

Overall, we can say that utility network restructuring is creating new contexts for the greening of consumption and provision at multiple levels and scales. However, rather than a shift from one paradigm to another, change is better understood as a process of partial reconfiguration in which old and new institutional and infrastructural logics and conventions interact. The overall result is a complex landscape encompassing highly variable opportunities for environmental renewal that are tempered by long-standing conventions and regulations.

Having considered these various dimensions of infrastructural change, we can now piece together a more systemic representation of what these mean for environmental innovation.

SYSTEMS OF 'CO-PROVISION'

The construction and management of utility systems is, at heart, a systemic process involving interactions between multiple consumers, providers and technologies. Conventional conceptual distinctions between consumers and providers, or between supply and demand management, fail to capture the socio-technical connectivities around which utilities are built.

What we offer here is an interpretation of utility system organization that recognizes its uniquely interdependent characteristics. Specifically, we argue that attempts to restructure utility systems involve processes of 'co-provision'. The notion of co-provision represents an important conceptual development; instead of viewing infrastructural and environmental change in terms of the 'bottom-up' greening of consumer choice or the 'top-down' greening of production, co-provision implies that sustainable modes of provision will be shaped by interactions between multiple supply-chain agencies. The idea that patterns of demand or supply are collectively structured has saliency with respect to all supply chains; but in network-based situations, relations between co-providers are often strengthened or weakened by particular technical linkages and interdependencies.

As shown in Chapter 4 (see Figure 4.1), traditional relations between consumers and providers are often conceptualized as a linear set of arrangements between the server (monopoly providers) and the served (captive consumers) – technologies being represented as 'fixes' to environmental problems. During the course of the book we have challenged the view that the environmental modernization of utility systems can be best achieved through focusing on the consumer end of supply chains or on the provider alone. Instead, we have developed a more 'systemic' approach that takes account of a much broader range of interactions and intermediaries implicated in the construction of new modes and scales of service provision and new configurations of demand and choice. Our re-conceptualized 'system of co-provision' details new utility-user relations that are, to some extent, reframing contexts for supply and demand management today. This approach is illustrated in Figure 8.1.

In Figure 8.1, consumers appear as captive consumers, customers, citizens and consumer-providers. Producer roles also take on multiple dimensions: green electricity or grey water production might now be co-managed by households and social housing providers or co-operatives, as well as by regional, national or multinational utilities. Multiple 'intermediary' providers might be responsible for aspects of distribution, disposal or supply.

Scales of social and technical organization are also highly variable and the boundaries or parameters of the system of co-provision might be expanded or reduced in order to reflect different dependencies on pan-European organizations, or on locally constructed mini-grids or home composting systems. Processes of environmental renewal might be instigated at multiple points so that a variety of mini-grids emerge alongside more mainstream arrangements. Within these sub-systems, approaches to demand-and-supply management reflect different institutional and political priorities, as well as varying technological possibilities.

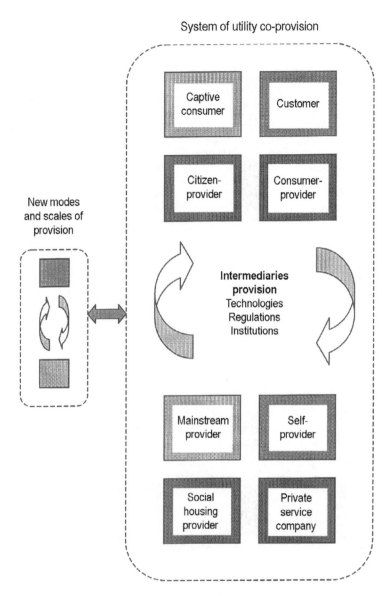

Figure 8.1 *Systems of co-provision*

In Figure 8.1, infrastructures and regulatory arrangements are depicted as a form of 'connective tissue' that structures and organizes the actions of co-providers. Occasionally, this might tie utility service providers into now outdated modes of provision or force them to rely upon old concepts of efficiency or optimality. Equally, new systems of regulation can be used to create a context in which utilities and users work together to co-manage demand.

Importantly, none of these arrangements imply the wholesale fragmentation or differentiation of utility systems. Instead, they indicate the partial reconfiguration of relations. What we have shown through our empirical analyses is a range of new intermediate arrangements in which different groupings of consumers and providers, and different supporting technical and institutional frameworks, are being constructed. In each of these new network arrangements concepts of sustainability, efficiency and demand management take on different meaning, depending upon the objectives of combinations of co-providers.

Although the representation of systems of co-provision shown in Figure 8.1 is relevant to the organization of energy, water or waste service provision, socio-technical characteristics and dynamics differ in each case. System-specific arrangements can shift the balance of demand or supply responsibilities or of power between consumers and providers. As our analyses have shown, different opportunities for storing, transporting or collecting resources have direct consequences for what utilities can do to manage the flow of resources and influence demand.

RECOGNIZING CONNECTIVITIES: IMPLICATIONS AND CHALLENGES

At the start of this book we suggested that moments of system breakdown offer a reminder of the extent to which the technologies and practices of utility providers and consumers are interdependent. The character and dynamics of these interdependencies – especially those related to forms of environmental renewal – have been examined and explored in our case studies of Dutch and British innovations in utility management.

The complications that arise from managing such interconnected systems are recognized by utility managers and by policy-makers. Yet, there remains a disjuncture between the conceptualization of network-based consumption and current approaches to environmental policy and practice. The challenge of sustainable provision is still largely regarded as one of promoting more efficient technologies and introducing a range of greener products and services for end-users. The logic of our argument is that this is not enough.

In this book, we have shown that it is important to acknowledge the spatial and temporal qualities of supply when analysing opportunities for demand management in electricity, water and waste systems. The resulting patchwork of available options depends upon the ability of diverse co-providers to renegotiate levels of acceptable risk, upon possibilities for overcoming localized load pressures by re-routing resource flows, and upon how regulatory frameworks support or inhibit these efforts. Organizational changes in ownership and responsibility influence the manner in which demand is configured; but exactly how this works out depends upon the specific material, spatial and temporal permutations around which networks are built.

Reinforcing existing networks is not the only possible response to infrastructural crises and concerns about security. New systems of co-provision might be built around principles of interrupted rather than continual supply. Mass and niche systems might be combined to form new configurations of central and local supply, and correspondingly novel ways of differentiating waste or managing peaks and flows. The experiences of those managing 'marginal' systems suggest that infrastructures can be organized on different scales. Likewise, the experiences of mainstream providers show that existing infrastructures can be operated and managed in significantly different ways should organizational priorities and procedures change. On both counts, infrastructures, which constitute the invisible backbone of everyday life, are more flexible – and, hence, more open to environmental renewal – than might at first appear.

References

Akrich, M. (1992) 'The de-scription of technical objects' in Bijker, W., Wiebe, E. and Law, J. (eds) *Shaping Technology/Building Society: Studies in Sociotechnical Change*, MIT Press, Cambridge, Mass

Arthur, W. (1989) 'Competing technologies, increasing returns and lock-in by historical events', *Economics Journal*, 99, pp116–131

Awerbuch, S. (2003) 'Decentralized electricity networks, mass-customization and intermittent renewables in the 21st century: Taking a giant step backwards', Draft paper for Tyndall Centre seminar, The Decarbonisation of Modern Societies, 22 October

Barton, H. (1998) 'Eco-neighbourhoods: A review of projects', *Local Environment*, 3 (2), June, pp159–177

Bauman, Z. (1990) *Thinking Sociologically*, Blackwell, Oxford

Berkhout, F. (2002) 'Technological regimes, path dependency and the environment', *Global Environmental Change*, 12, pp1–4

Berrie, T. (1992) *Electricity Economics and Planning*, Peter Peregrinus, London

Bhatti, M., Brooke, J. and Gibson, M. (1994) *Housing and the Environment: A New Agenda*, Chartered Institute of Housing, Coventry

Bijker, W. (1995) *Of Bicycles, Bakelites, and Bulbs: Toward a Theory of Sociotechnical Change*, MIT Press, London

Bläser, J. F. E. (1992) *Mensen en Spanningen, Sociaal-Economische Geschiedenis van de N. V. Provinciale Noordbrabantsche Electriciteitsmaatschappij 1914–1985*, Martinus Nijhoff, Leiden

Bourdieu, P. (1984) *Distinction: A Social Critique of Judgement and Taste*, Routledge, London

Boyle S. (1996) 'DSM progress and lessons in the global context', *Energy Policy*, 24 (4), pp345–359

Brown, P. and Cameron, L. (2000) 'What can be done to reduce overconsumption?', *Ecological Economics*, 32 (1), pp27–41

Bunker, S., Coates, C., How, J., Jones, L. and Morris, W. (1997) (eds) *Diggers and Dreamers – The Guide to Communal Living 98/99*, Diggers and Dreamers Publications, London, pp1–224

Campbell, C. (1998) 'Conceiving consumption: A survey of the frames of meaning commonly employed in the study of consumption', Paper presented at seminar on Consumption, Environment and Social Sciences, Oxford

Centre for the Environment, Ethics and Society, Mansfield College, Oxford, July

CDS Housing (1999) *Harlow Park 'Green' Handbook*, CDS Housing, Liverpool

Chappells, H. (2003) *Re-conceptualising Electricity and Water: Institutions, Infrastructures and the Construction of Demand*, PhD thesis, Lancaster University, Lancaster

Chappells, H., Klintman, M., Linden, A.-L., Shove, E., Spaargaren, G. and Van Vliet, B. (2000) *Domestic Consumption, Utility Services and the Environment*, Final report of the Domus Project (EU DGXII – ENV-CT97-0467), Wageningen University, Wageningen

Chappells, H. and Shove, E. (1999) 'The Dustbin: A study of domestic waste, household practices and utility services', *International Planning Studies*, 4 (2), pp267–280

Clark, M. (2001) 'Domestic futures and sustainable residential development', *Futures*, 33, pp817–836

Cohen, M. J. (1998) 'Science and the environment: Assessing cultural capacity for ecological modernization', *Public Understanding of Science*, 7 (2), pp149–167

Cooper G. (1998) *Air-conditioning America: Engineers and the Controlled Environment, 1900–1960*, John Hopkins University Press, Baltimore

Coutard, O. (1999) (ed) *The Governance of Large Technical Systems*, Routledge, London

Cowan, R. S. (1983) *More Work for Mother: The Ironies of Household Technology from the Open Hearth to the Microwave*, Basic Books, New York

David, P. A. (1985) 'Clio and the economics of QWERTY', *American Economic Reviews*, 75, pp332–337

De Laat, B. (1996) *Scripts for the Future*, PhD thesis, University of Amsterdam, Amsterdam

DETR (Department of the Environment, Transport and the Regions) (1998a) '10–point water plan', HMSO, London

DETR (Department of the Environment, Transport and the Regions) (1998b) Sustainable Development: Opportunities for Change, DETR, London

DOE (Department of the Environment) (1992) *Using Water Wisely*, Consultation paper, Department of the Environment, London

Douglas, M. and Isherwood, B. (1996) *The World of Goods: Towards an Anthropology of Consumption*, Routledge, London

Dunn, S. (2000) *Micropower: The Next Electrical Era*, Worldwatch Paper 151, Worldwatch Institute, Washington, DC

Ebreo, A., Hershey, J. and Vining, J. (1999) 'Reducing solid waste: Linking recycling to environmentally responsible behaviour' *Environment and Behaviour* 31 (1), pp107–135

EC (European Commission) (1999) *Sustainable Urban Development in the European Union: A Framework for Action*, www.ecotec.com/urbanissues/forum/src/ppaper03.htm

Eerste Kamer der Staten Generaal (2003) *Wijziging van de Waterleidingwet* (*eigendom waterleidingbedrijven*), Vergaderjaar 2003–2004, nr 28339, A, SDU, Den Haag

Ekins, P. (2003) Environment and Human Behaviour: A New Opportunities Programme, www.psi.org.uk/ehb/

Elzen, B., Geels, F. G. and Green, K. (2004) (eds) *System Innovation and the Transition to Sustainability: Theory, Evidence and Policy*, Edward Elgar Publishing, Cheltenham

Environment Agency (1998) *Resource Demand Management Techniques for Sustainable Development*, Environment Agency, Bristol

EST (Energy Saving Trust) (1994) *Recommendations on the Standards of Performance in Energy Efficiency for the Regional Electricity Companies*, EST, London

Estache, A. (1995) (ed) *Decentralizing Infrastructure: Advantages and Limitations*, Discussion Paper 290, Worldbank, Washington, DC

Evans, B. (1997) 'Designing EcoLite homes', *The Architects Journal*, 3 April

Fairlie, S. (1996) *Low Impact Development: Planning and People in a Sustainable Countryside*, Jon Carpenter Publishing, Charlbury

Fine, B. and Leopold, E. (1993) *The World of Consumption*, Routledge, London

Forty, A. (1986) *Objects of Desire: Design and Society, 1750–1980*, Cameron Books, London

Gandy, M. (1994) *Recycling and the Politics of Urban Waste*, Earthscan, London

Garrett, P. (1997) 'Who do we think we are?', *Utility Week*, 4 April, pp12–13

Gatersleben, B. and Vleck, C. (1998) 'Household consumption, quality of life and environmental impacts: A psychological perspective and empirical study' in Noorman, K. J. and Uitkeramp, T. S. (eds) *Green Households? Domestic Consumers, Environment and Sustainability*, Earthscan, London

Geels, F. and Kemp, R. (2000) 'Transities vanuit sociotechnisch perspectief', Achtergrondrapport voor het vierde Nationaal Beleidsplan (NMP–4), www.meritbbs.unimaas.nl/rkemp/geelskemp.pdf

Gellings, C. W. (1996) 'Then and now: the perspective of the man who coined the term "DSM" ', *Energy Policy*, 24 (4), pp285–288

Going for Green/Tidy Britain Group (1998) *Less Waste More Value*, Response to the consultation paper on the waste strategy for England and Wales, DETR, London

Gosling, P. (1996) 'The race for grid positions: councils may move into the energy business by selling surplus supplies', *The Independent*, 14 August

Graham, S. and Marvin, S. (1995) 'More than ducts and wires: Post-Fordism, cities and utility networks', in Healey, P. et al (eds) *Managing Cities: The New Urban Context*, Wiley, London, pp169–190

Graham, S. and Marvin, S. (2001) *Splintering Urbanism: Networked Infrastructures, Technological Mobilities and the Urban Condition*, Routledge, London

Greenpeace (1999) 'Doorbraak in Solaris-project', Press release, 14 March 1999

Guy, S., Graham, S. and Marvin, S. (1997) (eds) 'Splintering networks: Cities and technical networks in 1990s Britain', *Urban Studies*, 34 (2), pp191–216

Guy, S. and Marvin, S. (1995) *The Commodification of Water: New Logics of Water Management in Britain*, Working paper, University of Newcastle, Newcastle

Guy, S. and Marvin, S. (1996) 'Transforming urban infrastructure provision: The emerging logic of demand side management', *Policy Studies*, 17 (2), pp137–147

Guy S., Marvin S. and Moss T. (2001) *Urban Infrastructures in Transition: Networks, Buildings, Plans*, Earthscan, London

Guy, S. C. and Osborn, S. P. (1997) *The Social Construction of Green Buildings*, Proceedings of the 6th IRNES Conference on Technology, the Environment and Us, Imperial College, London, 22–23 September

Gwilliam, M., Bourne, C., Smain, C. and Prat, A. (1998) *Sustainable Renewal of Suburban Areas*, Joseph Rowntree Foundation, York

Haddon, L., Karl, I. and Mandeville, L. (1997) 'Intelligent and green housing: Consumer issues', *Report to the Integer Group*, October, pp37–76

Hannah L. (1979) *Electricity before Nationalisation: A Study of the Development of the Electricity Supply Industry in Britain to 1948*, Macmillan Press, London

Hannah L. (1982) *Engineers, Managers and Politicians: The First Fifteen Years of Nationalized Electricity Supply in Britain*, Macmillan Press, London

Hastoe Housing Association (1997) Affordable Water: A Report on the Need to Save Water and How This Can Be Practicably Achieved at Little Extra Cost, Hastoe Housing Association, Teddington

Hill, D. (1996) 'What a load of old rubbish', *The Observer*, 28 July, p12

Hodgson, S. (1997) 'Competing locally from 1998', *Energy in Buildings and Industry*, June, pp6–9

Holtsprake (1998) 1 (newsletter) De Bongerd, Zwolle

Hughes, T. P. (1983) *Networks of Power: electrification in Western society, 1880–1930*, The John Hopkins University Press, Baltimore

Hutton, W. (1998) 'Darkness at the heart of privatisation', *The Observer*, 8 March, p24

IPH (Informatiecentrum Preventie en Hergebruik) (1998) *Afvalpreventie door Huishoudens: projectenoverzicht*, IPH, Utrecht

Jackson, T. and Michaelis, L. (2003) *Policies for Sustainable Consumption: A Report to the Sustainable Development Commission*, London, www.surrey.ac.uk/eng/ces/research/policies.pdf

Jensen, J. O. (2001) 'Green buildings in an infrastructure perspective', in Guy, S. et al (eds) *Urban Infrastructure in Transition: Networks, Buildings, Plans*, Earthscan, London

Joerges, B. (1988) 'Large technical systems: Concepts and issues' in Mayntz, R. and Hughes, T. (eds) *The Development of Large Technical Systems*, Westview Press, Boulder, CO

Kaufmann, J. C. (1998) *Dirty Linen: Couples and Their Laundry*, Middlesex University Press, London

Kemp, R., Schot, J. and Hoogma, R. (1998) 'Regime shifts through processes of niche formation: The approach of strategic niche management', *Technology Analysis and Strategic Management*, 10 (2), pp175–196

King, J. (1997) (ed) *Family Spending – A Report on 1996–1997*, Family Expenditure Survey, Office of National Statistics, London, pp1–184

Künneke, R. W. (1999) 'Electricity networks: how "natural" is the monopoly?' *Utilities Policy*, 8, pp99–108

Latour, B. (1992) 'Where are the missing masses? The sociology of a few mundane artefacts', in Bijker, W. and Law, J. (eds) *Shaping Technology/ Building Society*, MIT Press, Cambridge, MA

Leversedge F. M. (1974) (ed) *Priorities in Water Management*, University of Victoria, Victoria, British Columbia

Lie, M. and Sorensen, K. (1996) (eds) *Making Technology Our Own? Domesticating Technology into Everyday Life*, Scandinavian University Press, Oslo

Lovins A. B. (1977) *Soft Energy Paths: Towards a Durable Peace*, Penguin Books, Harmondsworth

McEvoy, D., Gibbs, D. C. and Longhurst, J. W. S. (1999) 'The prospect for improved energy efficiency in the UK residential sector', *Journal of Environmental Planning and Management*, 42 (3), pp409–424

Melosi, M. (2000) *The Sanitary City: Urban Infrastructure in America from Colonial Times to the Present*, Johns Hopkins University Press, Baltimore

Ministry of Economic Affairs (1995) *Derde Energienota 1996*: White Paper, SDU, Den Haag

Ministry of Environment (1994) *Drinking Water in The Netherlands*, VROM, Den Haag

Ministry of Environment and Spatial Planning (1993) *Beleidsplan Drink – en Industriewatervoorziening*, SDU, Den Haag

Moisander, J. (1995) 'Consumers' pro-environmental attitudes and their use of public transportation', European Council for an Energy Efficient Economy, 1995

Summer Study Proceedings, www.eceee.org/library_links/proceedings/1995/ abstract/ece95066.lasso

Mol, A. P. J. and Spaargaren, G. (1992) 'Sociology, environment and modernity: Towards a theory of ecological modernization', *Society and Natural Resources*, 5 (4), pp323–344

Moss, T. (2000) 'Unearthing water flows, uncovering social relations: introducing new waste water technologies in Berlin', *Journal of Urban Technology*, 7 (1), pp63–84

Moss, T. (2004) 'Institutional restructuring, entrenched infrastructures and the dilemma of overcapacity', in Southerton, D., Chappells, H. and Van Vliet, B. (eds) *Sustainable Consumption: The Implications of Changing Systems of Provision*, Edward Elgar, Cheltenham

National Housing Forum (1997) *Living Places: Sustainable Homes, Sustainable Communities*, National Housing Forum, London, pp1–47

Noorman, K. J. and Uitkeramp, T. S. (eds) (1998) *Green Households? Domestic Consumers, Environment and Sustainability*, Earthscan, London

NRA (National Rivers Authority) (1994) *Water – Nature's Precious Resource*, HMSO, London

Nye, D. (1992) *Electrifying America: Social Meanings of a New Technology*, MIT Press, Cambridge, MA

O'Brien, M. (1999) 'Rubbish values: Reflections on the political economy of waste', *Science as Culture*, 8 (3), pp269–295

O'Conner, H. (1999) *Solway Water Conservation Scheme: Final Report and Results 1998/99*, North West Water Report (March), North West Water, Manchester

OECD (Organisation for Economic Co-operation and Development) (2002) *Towards Sustainable Household Consumption?: Trends and Policies in OECD Countries*, OECD, Paris

OFFER (Office of Electricity Regulation) (1998) *Energy Efficiency Standards of Performance for Public Electricity Suppliers, 1998–2000*, OFFER, Birmingham

OFFER (1992) *Demand Side Measures: A Report to the Office of Electricity Regulation by LE Energy and SRC International*, OFFER, Birmingham

OFWAT (Office of Water Regulation) (1997) *Report on Leakage and Water Efficiency 1996–1997*, OFWAT, Birmingham

OFWAT (2001) *Report on Leakage and the Efficient Use of Water, 2000–2001* (October), OFWAT, Birmingham

Ogle, M. (1996) *All the Modern Conveniences: American Household Plumbing, 1840–1890*, Johns Hopkins University Press, Baltimore

Osborn, S. and Marvin, S. (2001) 'Restabilizing a heterogeneous network: The Yorkshire drought, 1995–96', in Guy, S., Marvin, S. and Moss, T. (eds) *Urban Infrastructures in Transition: Networks, Buildings, Plans*, Earthscan, London

Otnes, P. (1988) (ed) *The Sociology of Consumption*, Humanities Press International, New Jersey

Parr, J. (1999) *Domestic Goods: The Material, The Moral and The Economic in the Postwar Years*, University of Toronto Press, Toronto

Patterson, W. (1990) *The Energy Alternative: Changing the Way the World Works*, Boxtree, London

Patterson, W. (2003) *Keeping the Lights On*, Working Paper No 1, The Royal Institute of International Affairs, London, www.riia.org/pdf/briefing_papers/The%20Electric%20Challenge%20Patterson%202003.pdf

Pezzey, J. C. V. and Mill, G. A. (1998) *A Review of Tariffs for Public Water Supply*, Environment Agency, London, UK

Post, M. (2000) 'Self-sufficiency: For environmental reasons or just for fun?', Paper presented at the ESF Winter Workshop Infrastructures of Consumption and the Environment, Wageningen, 25–27 November 2000

Powergen (2003) *Corporate Responsibilty Report 2003*, www.eon–uk.com/corporate_responsibility/reports/corporate_responsibility_report_2003

Raman, S., Chappells, H., Klintman, M. and Van Vliet, B. (1998) *Inventory of Environmental Innovations in Domestic Utilities: The Netherlands, Britain and Sweden*, Report for the Domus Project, Wageningen University, Wageningen

Redclift, M. (1996) *Wasted: Counting the Costs of Global Consumption*, Earthscan, London

Rees, J. A. (1974) 'Water management and pricing policies in England and Wales', in Leversedge, F. M. (ed) *Priorities in Water Management*, University of Victoria, Victoria, British Columbia

Reisch, L. (2001) 'Time and wealth: The role of time and temporalities for sustainable patterns of consumption', *Time and Society*, 10 (2/3), pp387–405

Remu (1999) 'Zonnepanelen systeem SunPower', www.remu.nl

Rip, A. and Kemp, R. (1998) 'Technological change', in Rayner, S. and Malone, E. (eds) *Human Choice and Climate Change: Resources and Technology*, vol2, Battelle Press, Columbus, Ohio

Roche, D. (2000) *A History of Everyday Things: The Birth of Consumption in France, 1600–1800*, Cambridge University Press, Cambridge

Røpke, I. (1999) 'The dynamics of willingness to consume', *Ecological Economics*, 28, pp399–420

Rotmans, J., Kemp, R. and Van Asselt, M. (2001) 'More evolution than revolution: Transition management in public policy', *Foresight*, 3 (1), pp15–31

Schot, J. and Rip, A. (1997) 'The past and future of constructive technology assessment', *Technological Forecasting and Social Change*, 54, pp251–268

Schumacher E. F. (1973) *Small Is Beautiful: A Study of Economics as if People Mattered*, Blond and Briggs, London

Sheail, J. (1991) *Power in Trust: The Environmental History of the CEGB*, Oxford University Press, Oxford

Shove, E. (1997) 'Notes on comfort, cleanliness and convenience', Paper for the ESF Workshop on Consumption, Everyday Life and Sustainability, Lancaster, 5–8 April 1997

Shove, E. (2003) *Comfort, Cleanliness and Convenience: The Social Organization of Normality*, Berg, Oxford and London

Shove, E. (2004) 'Changing human behaviour and lifestyle: A challenge for sustainable consumption?' in Røpke, I. and Reisch, L. (eds) *The Ecological Economics of Consumption*, Elgar, Cheltenham

Shove, E. and Chappells, H. (2001) 'Ordinary consumption and extraordinary relationships: Utilities and their users', in Gronow, J. and Warde, A. (eds) *Ordinary Consumption*, Routledge, London

Shove, E., Lutzenhiser, L., Guy, S., Hackett, B. and Wilhite, H. (1998) 'Energy and social systems', in Rayner, S. and Malone, E. (eds) *Human Choice and Climate Change: Resources and Technology*, vol 2, Battelle Press, Columbus, Ohio

Shove, E. and Warde, A. (2001) 'Inconspicuous consumption: The sociology of consumption, lifestyles, and the environment', in Dunlap, R., Buttel, F., Dickens, P. and Gijswijt, A. (eds) *Sociological Theory and the Environment: Classical Foundations, Contemporary Insights*, Rowman and Littlefield, Lanham, Maryland

Sioshansi, F. P. (1996) 'DSM in transition: From mandates to markets' *Energy Policy*, 24 (4), pp283–284

Sioshansi, F. P. and Davis, E. H. (1989) 'Information technology and efficient pricing: Providing a competitive edge for electric utilities' *Energy Policy*, 17 (6), pp599–607

Slingerland, S. (1999) *Energy Conservation and Electricity Sector Liberalisation: Towards a Green and Competitive Electricity Supply?*, PhD thesis, University of Amsterdam, Amsterdam

Southerton, D. (2000) 'Introduction', in Reader of the ESF Winter Workshop, *Infrastructures of Consumption and the Environment*, Wageningen University, Wageningen, 25–27 November 2000

Spaargaren, G. (1997) *The Ecological Modernization of Production and Consumption: Essays in Environmental Sociology*, PhD thesis, Landbouw Universitiet, Wageningen

Spaargaren, G. and Van Vliet, B. (2000) 'Lifestyles, consumption and the environment: The ecological modernization of domestic consumption', *Environmental Politics*, 9 (1), pp50–77

Stoter, P. (1994) 'Levert een waterleidingbedrijf alleen drinkwater of meer?', *H2O*, 27 (15), pp427–430

Strang, V. (2004) *The Meaning of Water*, Berg, Oxford

Strasser, S. (1982) *Never Done*, Pantheon, New York

Strasser, S. (2000) *Waste and Want: A Social History of Trash*, Metropolitan Books, New York

Summerton, J. (1994) (ed) *Changing Large Technical Systems*, Westview Press, Oxford

Summerton, J. (2004) 'The new "energy divide": Policies, social equity and sustainable consumption in changing infrastructures', in Southerton, D., Chappells, H. and Van Vliet, B. (eds) *Sustainable Consumption: The Implications of Changing Infrastructures of Provision*, Edward Elgar Publishing, Cheltenham

Sylvester, S. (1998) *Sociale Monitoring zonne-energieproject '114 SCW–woningen' Nieuwland Amersfoort*, Eindrapport, Erasmus University, Rotterdam

Tellegen, E. et al (1996) 'Nutsbedrijven en de Beperking van Huishoudelijk Milieugebruik', in Van Heerikhuizen et al (eds) *Milieu als Mensenwerk*, AST 23:1/ Wolters-Noordhoff, Groningen, pp 218–241

Thompson, M. (1979) *Rubbish Theory: The Creation and Destruction of Value*, Oxford University Press, Oxford

Trentmann, F. and Taylor, V. (2004) 'Liquid politics: Water politics in Victorian England and the formation of the consumer', www.consume.bbk.ac.uk/knowconsumer.html

Truffer, B., Voss, J.-P. and Konrad, K. (2002) 'Integrated microsystems of supply, anticipation, evaluation and shaping of transformation in the German utility sector', Paper for the EASST Conference on Responsibility under Uncertainty, 31 July–2 August, York, UK

Turton, P. (1995) 'Domestic consumption monitoring survey', *Report 5*, NRA Demand Management Centre

Tweede Kamer der Staten Generaal (1999) *Herziening Waterleidingwet*, Vergaderjaar 1999–2000, 25869, no 4, SDU, Den Haag

Tweede Kamer der Staten Generaal (2003) *Toepassing Huishoudwater*, Vergaderjaar 2002–2003, 26484, SDU, Den Haag

Tweede Kamer der Staten Generaal (2004) *Groene Stroom*, Rapport, Vergaderjaar 2003–2004, 29630, SDU, Den Haag

URBED (Urban and Economic Development Group) (1995) *21st Century Homes: Building to Last*, Report for the Joseph Rowntree Foundation, Joseph Rowntree Foundation, York

Utrechts Nieuwsblad (2000) 29 January

Uusitalo, L. (1990) 'Consumer preferences for environmental quality and other social goals', *Journal of Consumer Policy*, 13 (3), pp231–251

Vaessen, H. (1998) 'Huishoudwater Waterbedrijf Gelderland: Van pilot naar beleid', Paper for the Conference *Nationale Dubodag*, Amsterdam, 25 November

Van den Burg, S., Van Buuren, J. and Van Vliet, B. (1999) 'Huishoudwater: Een nieuwe standaard?' *H2O*, 32 (19), pp7–10

Van Mierlo, B. C. (1997) *De totstandkoming van twee grote Pilotprojecten met zonnecellen in nieuwbouwwijken, Een vergelijking tussen Amsterdam en Amersfoort*, IVAM, Amsterdam

Van Vliet, B. (1995) *Waterbesparing: over spoeling en verspilling*, Report 107, Liasion Office Wageningen University, Wageningen

Van Vliet, B. (2000) *Huishoudwater in Wageningen Noord-West*, Wageningen University, Wageningen

Van Vliet, B. (2002) *Greening the Grid: The Ecological Modernisation of Network Bound Systems*, PhD Thesis, Wageningen University, Wageningen

VEWIN (Vereniging van Waterbedrijven in Nederland) (2001) 'Water in Zicht 2000', Bedrijfsvergelijking in de Drinkwatersector, VEWIN, Rijswijk

Von Meier, A. (1994) 'Integrating supple technologies into utility power systems: Possibilities for reconfiguration', in Summerton, J. (ed) *Changing Large Technical Systems*, Westview Press, Oxford

Von Weizsäcker, E., Lovins, A. B. and Lovins, L. H. (1998) *Factor Four: Doubling Wealth, Halving Resources*, Earthscan, London

Wackernagel, M and Rees, W (1995) *Our Ecological Footprint*, New Society Publishers, Gabriola Island, BC

WCED (World Commission on Environment and Development) (1987) *Our Common Future: Report of the World Commission on Environment and Development*, The Brundtland Report, Oxford University Press, Oxford and New York

Winpenny, J. (1994) *Managing Water as an Economic Resource*, Routledge, London

Wolsink, M., Hertz, B. and Slingerland, S. (1998) *Utility Sectors in The Netherlands*, Report for the Domus project, University of Wageningen, Wageningen

Zelle, R. and Van der Zwaan, R. (1997) *Ervaringen met tariefdifferentiatie en huishoudelijk afval*, VROM, Den Haag

INTERVIEWS

WMO (Waterleiding Maatschappij Overijssel), Water Company, Mr Van den Berg, Zwolle, 29 January 1999

GWL (Gemeente Waterleidingen Amsterdam), Water Company, Mr Groot and Mrs Roels, Amsterdam, 12 March 1999

Nuon, Multi-utility Company, Mr Klijn and Mr Van der Ploeg, Wageningen, 23 February 1998

WEBSITES

De Bongerd (Zwolle, The Netherlands):
www.mmwz.nl/
De Kleine Aarde (The Netherlands):
www.dekleineaarde.nl
De Twaalf Ambachten (The Netherlands):
www.de12ambachten.nl/English/index%20english.html
Energy Research Centre of The Netherlands (The Netherlands):
www.ecn.nl
Het Groene Dak (The Netherlands):
www.groenedak.nl
Meerwind (The Netherlands):
www.meerwind.nl
National Sustainable Building Centre (The Netherlands):
www.dubo–centrum.nl
Powergen (UK):
www.powergen.co.uk
SolarBuzz (US):
www.solarbuzz.com

Index

For Product Safety Concerns and Information please contact our EU
representative GPSR@taylorandfrancis.com Taylor & Francis Verlag GmbH,
Kaufingerstraße 24, 80331 München, Germany

Printed and bound by CPI Group (UK) Ltd, Croydon, CR0 4YY
11/05/2025
01866585-0002